The Writing Life

The Writing Life

National Book Award Authors

Random House New York

ALL PROFITS FROM THE SALE AND LICENSING OF THIS BOOK WILL GO TO THE NATIONAL BOOK FOUNDATION, INC.

 Published in the United States by Random House, Inc., New York, and simultaneously in Canada by Random House of Canada Limited, Toronto.

Owing to space limitations, permission acknowledgments can be found on page 242.

Library of Congress Cataloging-in-Publication Data
The writing life / edited by Neil Baldwin and Diane Osen.
p. cm.
ISBN 0-679-76983-8
1. American literature—20th century—History and criticism—Theory, etc. 2. Authors, American—20th century—Interviews. 3. Authorship. I. Baldwin, Neil. II. Osen, Diane.
PS221.W75 1996
810.9'0054—dc20 95-42500

Manufactured in the United States of America on acid-free paper

9876543

Book design by Wynn Dan

So why do I write, torturing myself to put it down? Because in spite of myself I've learned some things. Without the possibility of action, all knowledge comes to one labeled "file and forget," and I can neither file nor forget. Nor will certain ideas forget me; they keep filing away at my lethargy, my complacency. Why should I be the one to dream this nightmare? Why should I be dedicated and set aside–yes, if not to tell at least a few people about it? There seems to be no escape.

Ralph Ellison
Invisible Man
(National Book Award, 1953)

Contents

Photographs by CHRISTOPHER BIERLEIN ■ Interviews by DIANE OSEN

THE WRITING LIFE
SPONSORED BY THE NATIONAL BOOK FOUNDATION

Introduction

For Louis Begley, it was the sound of his mother's voice as she read to him. For John Updike, it was the sight of his mother at her typewriter. For Gloria Naylor, it was the touch of her mother's hand, offering the gift of a journal.

Of course, not every parent can nurture the writing life of a child, and not every child who hears a story, or watches one grow, or smooths down the pages of a brand-new diary, decides to embrace a life of reading and writing books. And while many authors can name their initial sources of inspiration, they cannot explain exactly why these experiences so utterly transformed them.

The Writing Life does not penetrate that mystery, either; but it does illuminate some of the dreams and desires that have shaped the *writing lives* of some of America's most influential novelists, poets, biographers, and historians. Here, in essays and interviews created for the National Book Foundation's "Writing Life" project, American authors recount the various ways in which they found their vocations and developed their distinctive voices. Not surprisingly, the stories they tell are as compelling as the works that have earned them international recognition as National Book Award winners and finalists.

Poet Philip Levine recalls composing his first poem at the age of fourteen, inspired by the flowering of a mock-orange bush he purchased with money earned washing windows: "I looked on the works my hands had wrought, then I said in my heart, As it happened to the gardener, so it happened to me, for we all go into one place; we are all earth and return to earth. The dark was everywhere, and as my voice went out I was sure it reached the edges of creation."

But Philip Levine did not decide to become a poet until many years later, he realized. In a 1993 interview, he said he wanted to write for "the people I grew up with who brothered, sistered, fathered and mothered me. Their presence seemed utterly lacking in the poetry I inherited at age 20, so I've spent the last 40-some years trying to add to our poetry what wasn't there."

Novelist Gail Godwin, on the other hand, never considered any career but writing, having grown up watching her mother compose short stories and newspaper articles. But that certainty has never made living her writing life any easier. "I confess," she says, "to the doubts–and sometimes the outright *dreads*–that go with me as I climb the stairs to my study in the morning, coffee mug in hand: I have to admit to the habitual apprehension mixed with a sort of reverence,... as I wonder, what is going to happen today? *Will* anything happen? Will the angel come?"

The angel, she goes on to explain, "presides in that mysterious slice of time between when I *don't know what I am going to write that day* and when I'm looking afterward at the evidence of *what I did write that day.*"

The National Book Foundation's "Writing Life" project, which inspired this anthology, was designed to introduce readers across the country to the many manifestations of the angel Gail Godwin describes so vividly.

Since the project's inception five years ago, thousands of students and adults have joined together with more than one hundred National Book Award authors to consider how–and why –the gap is bridged between "I don't know" and "what I did write."

Meeting in schools, libraries, prisons, community centers, museums, senior-citizen centers, and other institutions large and small, in cities, suburbs, and rural towns, project participants have formed new groups dedicated to exploring the writing life and some of the unforgettable books it has engendered.

For example, from 1993 to 1995, participants in National Book Award Reading Circles had the opportunity to read twelve works of fiction, nonfiction and poetry recognized by the Awards and linked by shared concerns. Guided by scholars selected by cosponsoring State Humanities Councils, the Reading Circle members–including adults, high school and college students, teachers, professional writers, librarians and senior citizens–met to analyze the challenges of "creating a character" and "writing about families." Their discussions culminated in two-day residencies by National Book Award authors, who also traveled to other venues for larger public presentations under the auspices of the National Book Foundation.

What these authors learned along the way is embodied in this unique volume. We are immeasurably grateful to them for allowing us to share their extraordinary insights.

No introduction to this book would be complete without an expression of thanks to Random House, which will donate all its profits from the sale and licensing of this anthology to the foundation for the expansion of the "Writing Life" project; to the Lila Wallace–Reader's Digest Fund, which generously provided major funding for the project from its inception, as well as ongoing support; to the Federation of State Humanities Councils and the Library of Congress's Center for the Book, which did a masterful job of organizing scores of project events; and especially to the readers in forty states whose deep and abiding interest in the writing life has served as inspiration for us all.

NEIL BALDWIN, *Executive Director*
DIANE OSEN, *Director of Special Projects*
The National Book Foundation

The writer's desk

Rituals and Readiness: Getting Ready To Write

Gail Godwin

A woman gets up before dawn—it has to be before there is even that band of orange on the horizon—and lights a candle and walks about her house. If she waits until sunrise and it's too late to light the candle, she knows she won't write well that day.

A man has rented a house in Provence in order to write a novel. Every morning he retreats to a room of this house, and sits down at a small table, benumbed and mindless for several hours. His wife starts leaving a fresh rose on his table every morning, as a talisman of love and encouragement, but nothing helps. No words come.

A woman climbs the stairs of her house, closes the door, adjusts the blinds, lights two sticks of incense, the long, always-slightly crooked one handmade by a Tibetan monk, the neat, straight short one mass-produced at a factory in Tokyo. As the mixed aroma of musk, saffron, and sandalwood begins to permeate the room—a scent she has come to associate with the sacredness of work time—she turns on the computer and is always amazingly cheered by its booting-up noises. It and the printer to which it is attached make sweet, hopeful, familiar blumps and beeps, as if to say: we're here, we're warming up, we're checking out our parts, just as you are: we're going to HELP you today.

A man lies for three hours on his sofa, "sleepless and apathetic." On another day, he plays with his hair in front of a mirror. On another, washes his hands three times in succession and records it in his diary. Records on another day: "Complete standstill." On another, "Unending torments." On another, "Incapable in every respect." On another: "Another ten days and I have achieved nothing." On another, "In the afternoon I couldn't keep myself from reading what I had written yesterday. 'Yesterday's filth.' Didn't do any harm though."

And on another: "The possibility of serving with all one's heart."

What all of these people have in common is that their main job in life is writing fiction. The highly personal, sometimes agonizing, rituals I have just described them putting themselves through are their various and eccentric ways of warming up, of getting themselves worthy of entering that place where work will be done. It's that mysterious space each of us who writes must always enter–and engage with–in order to return with words. Much of the activity we think of as writing is, actually, *getting ready to write.*

I've been writing almost every day for thirty years, if you count newspaper jobs, then travel writing, then attempts at novels that never got published, then graduate school term papers, then more novels which *did* get published. I'm a person who has been in the habit of transposing her mental and emotional circuitry into words since the age of six or seven, first for grammar school purposes, then for letter and diary purposes, then for high school and college purposes.

And, as I begin to formulate my description of how one goes into this mysterious space where one writes, I find myself assailed by the same doubts that I cope with on an average morning when I go up to write my novel...when I go up to write *anything,* including this essay.

I confess, right at the start, to the doubts–and sometimes outright *dreads*–that go with me as I climb the stairs to my study in the morning, coffee mug in hand: I have to admit to the habitual apprehension mixed with a sort of reverence, as I light the incense–yes, I'm the one with the incense–and wonder: what is going to happen today? *Will* anything happen? Will the angel come today?

I could borrow from the experience of one of my own characters, in a novel I wrote fifteen years ago, as *she* embarks–for the first time in many years–on that process of finding words for what she truly means.

Here is Lydia Strickland Mansfield, the youngest daughter in *A Mother and Two Daughters.* She's in her late thirties in this chapter, the mother of two teenage sons, and recently separated from her husband. She's just returned to college, after a hiatus of twenty years, and she is in the throes of setting out to write a term paper for her most interesting course. This course, taught by a woman she admires and whose respect she wants to win, is called "The History of Female Consciousness." Lydia has chosen erotic love as the theme for her term paper, because, having recently begun a love affair, it is much on her mind. She has titled her paper "Eros: Friend or Foe."

So far, so good.

My ulterior motive as a novelist was to use Lydia's struggle with her term paper as the *shape* for this chapter which belongs solely to her. Lydia's grappling with *the paper's* ideas is to be the vehicle through which she processes–and, in so doing, reveals to the reader–her experiences and beliefs about romantic love and what she has been taught to expect from life in general. And out of these realizations, achieved as she struggles with her term paper and keeps digressing into reveries sparked by the subject matter–out of these realizations will come a better understanding of who and what she is. And a keener vision of what kind of world she's actually living in–built from her own observations, not secondhand ones.

Which, when you think about it, is a prime reason for writing. To better understand who and what we are and in what kind of place we're actually living. Built from our own observations; not secondhand ones.

> "We were brought up believing it is possible to find everything in one man," Lydia wrote in her neat, flowing hand across the yellow page. "My generation grew into womanhood certain that if we were nice-looking and chaste and pleasing in manner and dress, that Mr. Right would come and marry us and satisfy all our desires. He would take over our father's functions in caring for us, he would be an intellectual equal (or superior), and he would be the perfect lover."
>
> She read over what she had written. It flowed nicely, but was it a little too glib? Did it fall too much into the currently popular ruts of blame? ("Look what a mess we're in because they told us all *they* lies.") But how else should she start it? She looked at her watch and realized she had wasted almost an hour getting started. She began to panic, as she used to, long ago, whenever she had to write a book report for school. One night she had worked herself into hysterics because she couldn't get the first sentence of her book report. Daddy had taken her downstairs to his study and sat her down on his leather sofa with a soft, sharp pencil and one of his brand-new legal pads. "Now all you have to do is write me down one true thing about that book," Daddy said. "I haven't read it, so anything you can tell me about it will be of interest. Don't think of what your teacher expects you to write, or what you think you should write. Just write down one true thing about that book."
>
> Ever since that night, Lydia had always used legal pads and soft lead pencils, sharpened to stabbing points, when she had to write something.
>
> Was what she had written true? Well, yes and no. She was not exactly "brought up believing" those things, but, all the same, she had expected them...

> ...She read her paragraph over once again, hoping to spring from the momentum of its final words to her next idea. "...and he would be the perfect lover..."

Unlike Lydia, I never had a lawyer-father who sat me on his leather couch and provided me with a soft, sharp pencil and a brand-new legal pad and told me to write "one true thing" about whatever I had to write about, yet I do sharpen my pencils every single morning before I begin to write, even though I've worked on a word processor since 1989, and a typewriter for decades before that. I have to have those four or five stabbing points of soft, black lead, and the legal pad, lying handy to the right of my keyboard.

Now what did Leonard Strickland *mean* when he told Lydia to "write me down one true thing about that book"? What did he mean by "one true thing"? I created Leonard Strickland, so I ought to know what he meant, oughtn't I?

Well, I know that Leonard Strickland is a great admirer of Ralph Waldo Emerson, so he would undoubtedly be familiar with this passage from Emerson's essay on self-reliance:

> A man should learn to detect and watch that gleam of light which flashes across his mind from within, more than the luster of the firmament of bards and sages. Yet he dismisses without notice his thought, because it is his. In every work of genius we recognize our own rejected thoughts.

So: after the door is closed and the pencils have been sharpened to vanishing point and the empty pad lies ready and waiting...and the computer has been turned on and has put itself though its own little bleeping ceremony of checking out its circuits and reminding itself what it is capable of...and after a few more private rituals have been performed by me, how long do I have to wait for "that gleam of light which flashes across [my] mind from within" and is going to set me to writing that first sentence, that first "true thing"?

But what if that first true thing has *already* flashed through my mind–darted in and out quick as a swallow darting in and out of a barn?

For, often, don't you–when you're starting out to write something–"dismiss without notice," as Emerson put it, a thought *because it is merely yours*? You get just this split-second side-glimpse, a tantalizing flash of wings, before you reject it categorically. "No," you say, "that couldn't have been a swallow–much less an angel..." And you return safely to your glumness and panic and low opinion of yourself.

As Kafka put down his pen, and went to play with his hair in the mirror, and washed his hands three times...and returned to record in his diary: "Complete standstill...incapable in every respect...have achieved nothing."

Who is this critic within us who keeps assuring us we have glimpsed neither swallow nor angel, and even if we imagine we have, it's not worth recording because it would be only ours?

Let me introduce him to you. Or rather, let me introduce you to *my* inner critic, so that you may recognize from him some aspects of your own. I call him my Watcher at the Gate, and have written about him in an essay by that title.

I first realized I *had* a Watcher when I was leafing through Freud's *Interpretation of Dreams* some years ago. Ironically, it was my Watcher who had sent me to Freud in the first place. A character in my novel was having a dream and I lost confidence in my ability to give her the dream she needed, so I rushed to "an authority" to check out whether she ought to have such a dream. And, thanks to my angel, I found instead the following passage.

Freud is quoting from the poet Schiller, who is writing a letter to a friend. The friend has been complaining to Schiller about his own lack of creative power. Schiller tells him it's not good when the intellect examines too closely the ideas pouring in at the gates. In isolation, Schiller explains, an idea may be quite insignificant, and venturesome in the extreme, but it may acquire importance from an idea *which follows it*.

"In the case of a creative mind, it seems to me," Schiller goes on, "the intellect has withdrawn its watchers from the gates, and the ideas rush in pell-mell, and only then does it review and inspect the multitude. You are ashamed of the momentary and passing madness which is found in all real creators, the longer or shorter duration of which distinguishes the thinking artist from the dreamer...you reject too soon and discriminate too severely."

So that's what I had: a Watcher at the Gate. I decided to get to know him, and I have. I have written notes to him and he has replied. I even drew a portrait of him once.

Punctual to a fault, he always arrives ahead of me and is waiting for me in my study. The touching thing is, he's on my side. He doesn't want me to fail. He couldn't bear it. It would be so humiliating for both of us. So he is constantly cautioning me against recklessness and excesses, some of which might lead to brilliance. He is partial to looking out the window, looking for a wrinkle in the rug, looking up words. He adores looking up things, any kind of research. And before I had my computer, he was always advising me to stop in the middle of a typewritten page and type it over. "The neatness will re-establish the flow," he explained to me solemnly, wringing his hands—a favorite gesture of his.

That's my daily regular, who has been with me, looking exactly the same, since I first drew his portrait in 1976 (rather than get on with that morning's work). He's thin, with a willowy, ethereal stance; his hands are clasped tightly before him; he has abnormally round eyes, gazing slightly to his right—my left—bushy eyebrows, a fastidious little mustache and prissy lips. He has all his hair and it's still black. It's beginning to worry me that it's still so black, because he's somewhere between fifty and sixty and it would embarrass me to think he dyes it. He wears a black suit and a black tie. The only *sportif* note is the tightly buttoned collar of a dark plaid shirt peeping out above his lapels. I used to wonder whether he might be a clergyman, but couldn't settle on what denomination. More likely he's a bachelor scholar, with a neat little house full of antiques, who reads edifying books with his supper, committing to memory instructive passages to intimidate or slow me down the next day.

I don't know what this says about me, but I have become rather fond of my Watcher and sometimes think I have learned to work so well *in spite of him* that I wouldn't know what to do if he failed to show up one morning.

The other presence who inhabits the mysterious space in which we go to write is, of course, the angel. I first heard about another person's angel from the late painter Philip Guston. I asked him what he did on the mornings he didn't feel inspired. He said he usually went to his studio anyway. "And then I'll find myself thinking, well, I've got some of this pink paint left, so I'll brush some of it on and see what happens. And sometimes the angel comes. But what if I hadn't gone to my studio that day, and the angel *had* come?"

In my experience, the angel *does,* almost always, come. If I keep faith. On some days, keeping faith means simply *staying there,* when more than anything else I want to get out of that room. It sometimes means going up *without hope* and *without energy* and simply acknowledging my barrenness and lighting my incense and turning on my computer. And, at the end of two or three hours, and *without hope* and *without energy,* I find that I have indeed written some sentences that wouldn't have been there if I hadn't gone up to write them. And–what is even more surprising–these sentences written without hope or energy often turn out to be just as good as the ones I wrote *with* hope and energy.

So for me, the angel presides in that mysterious slice of time between when *I don't know what I'm going to write that day* and when I'm looking afterward at the evidence of *what I did write that day.*

Sometimes the best thing you can do is say: I've gone as far as I can. I'm empty. You might even pick up your diary and write, as Kafka did: "Complete standstill. Incapable in every respect." Or your own version of the above. "I can go no further," perhaps.

And then wait.

The German poet Rilke wrote two of his *Duino Elegies* and then lapsed into an almost decade-long depression. And then suddenly "utterance and release" came to him again. In only eighteen days he wrote the *Sonnets to Orpheus* and the remaining eight of his *Duino Elegies.* In the *Elegies,* the predominant symbol is the angel. The angel, for Rilke, as he explained to his Polish translator, is that creature in whom the actual and the ideal are one. Being in the angel's presence, for Rilke, meant being able to give the highest possible significance to our moments as they pass. And works of art, he further testifies, "are always products of having been in danger. Of having gone to the very end of an experience, to where one can go no further."

To where one can go no further. That is often the very point at which we issue our most irresistible invitation to the angel.

Take the man sitting in front of the small table in the house he has rented in France for a year to write a novel, and then finds he has nothing to say. The man whose wife, Sophie, leaves a rose on his barren table every morning. But no words come. The rest of the story, which was told to me by the novelist Jack Hawkes–he's written about this experience in his collection *Humors of Blood and Skin*–goes like this. One day a Frenchwoman in the village invites Jack and his wife for lunch, and Sophie insists that they go although Jack doesn't want to. Their hostess, to cheer up the depressed writer, begins recounting some tasty village gossip about a man in Nice who goes to pick up his daughter at school only to learn that she works as a prostitute in the afternoons. This anecdote sparked off two associative recollections in Hawkes's memory, and, at the end of his year in Provence, our writer came home with the manuscript of his novel, *The Passion Artist,* woven from the strands of the Frenchwoman's lunchtime story and the two essential recollections sparked by it.

In this case, the writer seemed to have to empty himself out, and admit–over and over again, as he faced his wife's fresh rose each day–that he was indeed empty. And wait. And not only wait, but go out to lunch. When the angel, disguised as a chatty Frenchwoman, would bring him the word.

Waiting for the word is what it's mostly about. Once, when Toni Morrison and I were on a TV program together, I asked her if she had any rituals.

She is the woman who has to get up before dawn, when she's at home, and light a candle and walk about the house.

I told her about my incense, and the sharpened pencils, and how, as soon as I turn off the green NumLock signal on my computer, I always touch a little religious medallion given to me by my mother. It's nailed to the window frame beside my computer.

"You know what all this is, don't you?" she said, smiling. "We're making our space unsecular. So we can receive the *word.*"

"Getting ready to write" doesn't apply just to *beginning* something: rituals, ways we coax ourselves into readiness, are equally as important for our *endings.*

Here's one last story. I wrote and asked my friend John Irving about *his* rituals. I said I knew he must have developed some special tactics for concentration during all those years when he was producing novels at home while his children were growing up.

"You're right," he wrote back, "children have largely informed what routine or ritual for writing that I have...My children have actually helped me to be resourceful about finding secretive ways to do this." Then he related the following example of one day's resourcefulness:

"I finished *The World According to Garp* on a day when both Colin and Brendan were home from school because there was a snowstorm and school was canceled. Two of their friends were visiting, and as I was trying the last paragraph for the third or fourth time that morning, a fight broke out over a Monopoly game and Brendan came crying to me for the solution to whatever injustice had befallen him...Colin had taken all his money or robbed all his hotels or sold all his railroads, and then hit him in the nose with the dice.

"I went and got a stove-timer from the kitchen and set it on the Monopoly board I set it at sixty minutes, and placed it in the middle of the Monopoly board. I said, 'Here are the rules. No fighting. Anyone who has a fight in the next hour must give the other players all his houses and hotels and money; anyone who loses all his hotels or houses or money in the next hour will have his money replaced by the bank, provided he hasn't been fighting. In one hour *I will play with you...'* (I *never* played Monopoly) '...and anyone who causes me to lose my houses or hotels or money will win five dollars of *real money*!!!'

"Thus they played silently and relentlessly for one hour, and in that time I finished the last paragraph to my satisfaction and readied myself to play Monopoly for the remainder of a long and snowy day. Colin won the $5 of real money, which I lost intentionally of course—as a way of eliminating myself from the game. Then I went back to my desk and rewrote the last paragraph. Of course, all the time I was losing the Monopoly game, I was thinking of the last paragraph, and I believe that the time away from my desk was a valuable part of that last paragraph, which I might have written too quickly without the sizeable interruption.

"I suppose this is just a way of saying that I find distractions useful because I have never lived a life where it is possible to eliminate them; therefore, I incorporate them."

Hamden, Connecticut, 1993

GAIL GODWIN is the author of nine novels, including *The Odd Woman, Violet Clay,* and *A Mother and Two Daughters,* which were National Book Award finalists; two collections of short stories, and four libretti.

Parkside: Writing from Love and Grief and Fear

Sandra Scofield

My daughter calls from Manhattan. “I miss the kitchen. I miss the cat on the sill, the light on your desk, the colors of the warp strung on my loom.” She is studying art. She knows that I like lists. She grew up making them.

> *Things to do:* Make Rice Krispie candy. Play Strawberry Shortcake Dolls. Go to the store with Mommy.
> *Ways you were mean to me last night:* You sent me to my room. You wouldn’t talk about it. You squeezed my elbow.

I love the kitchen, too. It is where I work, and where I often sit in the company of the cat, and of course it is where I cook, trying, when I do, to make up for the times I don’t. “What are we having?” my husband, Bill, asks when he sees me in an apron, bustling, with “that look” that says it isn’t an old standby, it isn’t soup or left-overs, it isn’t takeout. He sees that I’ve come back from wherever it is I go when I’m working. We fit in our dialogue about the irrigation pump, and the paint blistering on the south side of the house, the dog’s cataracts, and a neighbor’s sudden profusion of tulips. These small intimacies are essential. Sometimes

I talk about what my characters are doing; if you heard us you might think I was mentioning family or friends. I am buoyed by dailiness, both real and of my invention. I am cheered by the whiteness of my house.

I grew up in rented houses and trailers, and I still can't believe my luck. Ours is a small house, a mere thirty by thirty feet, but it has a broken roofline that keeps it from looking like a box, and a livingroom-kitchen with a nice arched ceiling like a picture I saw in *Metropolitan Home.* I'd still like a screened back porch, but who says I won't get it later? Anything can happen.

Our first house, across the valley near wheatfields and pear orchards, was larger. We needed more space then. Bill's son lived with us; now he's grown and gone. His girls used to come in the summer, till they grew adolescent, sulky; none of them have ever set foot in this house.

The idea to build a new, smaller house came one day a few years after my brother-in-law was murdered. All at once, there was in our house everything I wanted to leave behind, colors (brown, blue, orange) and space and history. Ahead there was the clean simplicity of a small house in a new place, and, I think now, the idea of myself as a writer. Once I got the idea, things moved fast. My husband, ever the boon companion, loves the bustle of large events, though he says he would never get another divorce or a new profession. When we decided we needed a new car, after nine years with the Subaru, he was like a boy in love, running all over, looking for the best deal. And when I posed the possibility of my return to teaching, if we could go overseas, that was good for months of perusing atlases and travel guides. We got as far as filling out the forms for an international schools service, but we never sent them in. At fifty dollars an application, you want to be sure. When it got right down to it, I couldn't imagine myself in a classroom again; I couldn't imagine myself in charge. Besides, I have these days; what would I do on one of them? Now, when one comes, I make myself get up, unless it's raining hard. If there is light, I sit in the kitchen doing nothing. I move when the light shifts. I go from the desk to the table. I begin a poem, a story–two lines, three. It takes all morning. I like the white expanse of my formica desk, clean as a hospital counter, and the sun in the morning. I read that artificial light relieves certain kinds of depression. When it is winter dark, people fold into lethargy, and then despair. They don't always make it to spring. Of course, real light is better. That's why I get up now. I realized what I was missing.

I only saw Bill's brother Bob two times, once with his wife. Two times too many, I always thought, even after he was dead. He made my skin prickle with dislike. He was good-looking, brash, with the frantic steady rap of a speed freak. The first time, he barged in on us when we were living in a condemned house in Helena. He had driven straight through from San Francisco, dressed in jungle fatigues. He was wild with exhaustion. He had felt, suddenly, that he had to go get a Montana deer. My husband dropped everything to go hunting with him, but would not go out a second day. He discovered that Bob didn't have a tag. Hunters are accused of so many wrongs. At least, he says, they should be careful to comply with the law.

Bob must have been the terrible burden in his mother's life, more so than his father, who drank too much but always came home and hung around even if he didn't have much to say. From early on, she must have imagined the trouble Bob might find. She must have worried about what would become of him, though she never thought of him soaked in his own blood on his workshop floor.

I putter through my days. The real work is at night. I always write late, sometimes all night, especially when I am closer to finishing than beginning a new piece. I am asked, where do you get your ideas? I think they find me. Joyce Carol Oates has written about "the phenomenon of being haunted, akin to love..." What one has lost, or never had, feeds the work. There is a chance to make things right, to explain and explore, and aided by memory and its transmutation, find a new place where I have not been and did not know I wished to go.

"Oh God, poor Momma," Bill said when she called to say Bob was dead. "She'll never get over this." I always liked it that he called her Momma. His parents were originally from West Texas, where I grew up, and there were lots of ways he and I shared a common culture because of it, though we grew up at opposite ends of the Great Plains.

His mother was stiff and pretend-friendly with me for a long time, though we get along well enough now. It's all long-distance, and I find that in letters you can make things whatever you wish them to be. Once when we went to see her, the first year we were married, I found a letter from Bill's ex-wife in the crack between the cushion and the arm of my chair. His ex-wife said it was all sex, and we deserved each other. She said he would be sorry, and she was sorry, too, that his mother had to see him act like this. What she really meant was, she would be sure he was as sorry as she could make him; and she did good job of it, because of the children. It wasn't me she hurt. I have Bill.

All Bill ever said about Bob was that they weren't anything alike. Bill had had so little contact with Bob as an adult, Bob hung somewhere back there in childhood, before helicopters in Vietnam or ambulances in San Francisco, or dope deals all over. It used to be, Bill would not talk about the past at all. Now I think it's that for years, when he looked back over his shoulder, all he could see was his ex-wife. Only lately has he begun telling me stories about his boyhood. He remembers details quite specifically, and I admire the way he knows the right word for every object, when my own world has always been a fuzzy generic one where most things exist without names, as blocks of color or emotion, or as background for events. When I am writing, I look everything up; card games and the names of trees, the symptoms of diseases.

Bill grew up in a small town where the range of economic classes was narrow, so he didn't realize that there were people who had it better than he did, and he seems to have liked his young life just fine. His mother was never strict about how he spent his time. She must have wondered, how much trouble can there be in a town of two thousand people? Bill laughs and tells me how the boys built paths up the side of a high hill and rode their bicycles off in a great arc. They built cannons out of pipes, and shot green plums powered by firecrackers.

I laugh too at these stories. I encourage him. I waited a lot of years to get him talking. Part of me, though, resents the picture he paints, even with Bob in it, getting into trouble when you would think there was none to be found. What I think gets to me in these tales of Bill's youth is that he doesn't seem to have had a hint–not even now, when he teaches kids he complains haven't the slightest sense of irony–of the malice and terror other children experience.

I lived as a child in my grandmother's house on Lamar, in Wichita Falls, Texas. She had a neighbor whose house was like a great southern mansion to us children. We dared one another to stick our feet across the property line, to touch toe to the neighbor's smooth stickerless grass. His house was white, with columns, and that lawn like a putting green, and all this on a street that was dirt, with big potholes and flash floods in rainstorms, as though it were some desert arroyo. The man whose house it was had once owned all the land around. He owned grocery stores in Colored Town, where he stocked giant bottles of vanilla extract to sell for the alcohol it contained. He shot a little kid–I think he was eight or nine–for playing on his yard one day at dusk; and he got away with it, because the boy was trespassing, and property is a cornerstone of decent life. I used to play with a girl on that street who had a cleft palate. Her parents, who were Assembly of God, believed it was the mark of God put on her for their sins, and they wouldn't have it repaired, even when a service organization offered to pay for everything. Between my grandmother's house and the bus stop, the small area where I was allowed to roam, I knew children whose fathers beat them with razor straps, and a girl who wasn't allowed to leave her house except to go to school or church. My own mother was crazy enough for shock treatments, pills, my family's constant watchful eye, and, finally, early death. I grew up thinking it was Texas that gave my family so much bad luck. I couldn't wait to leave. Somehow, the burden my mother was had not eased when she died. My grandmother hoarded her few possessions and never spoke of her, and, I thought, watched me for signs of madness. I woke many nights from dreams I wanted to abandon. But I was an optimist then. I thought it was a mere matter of geography. I thought I could leave bad luck behind.

All my life there have been days of sadness, vast featureless plains of it, like what Vásquez de Coronado saw when he first traversed what is now Texas. His men drove stakes into the buffalo grass so that they could make their way back. I once married a man with no faith in the future, and he died. Then I married for love and consolation and the pleasures of a modest life. Now I clip articles and keep a journal, though haphazardly. I tell myself there is no persistent evil, though we are each alone. I know it's just the level of serotonin put out by the brain. I know that light helps, and that you have to wait it out. I have so many reasons to be happy. Though the plains reach out endlessly, so that you seem to drown in space, beneath them are innumerable lakes and streams, the cold pure force of water; and if you can tap that water, however fierce the land above, you can live.

Bob married a flower-child in Haight-Ashbury, where he ran a tree store and lived on donations and sideline dealing. After some bad times, his wife's family moved them onto property they were buying, right on the Oregon–California border, ninety minutes from us. Bob called Bill collect to invite us down. It was June and still cold. The property was a rundown seedy ring of tourist cabins in a dark wet hollow. Bob was supposed to be fixing it up for summer business in return for living in one of the shacks. He said they couldn't eat if he had not made a couple of last-minute deals before he moved on. I had heard something about his deals. He kept us up late that first night on his Montana visit, telling us about a scheme gone sour, when he had thought he was about to buy the farm. He grinned as he said, "buy the farm," enjoying how dumb it sounded when we could all see he was really hip. It seemed he had not met his end of an agreement, a simple mistake, not intended, but the other party said he was greedy. There was a confrontation, a mortal threat. He got out of it by thinking fast and being bold. He said he grabbed the man's ear really hard. When the assailant got away–he had dropped his gun in surprise and pain–Bob was left holding the ear. He said. So now he had a little cash, an old GMC pickup, and a cute three-year-old boy they called Peewee. His wife was reading *The Tao of Pooh.* She wanted her son to grown up in peace, she said, as if peace were a county near the coast. I thought she was daffy and paranoid. She would not let Peewee play with any of the kids along the highway where they lived because she did not want their mothers to come to her place. She would not let him go with anybody except Bob or her parents, not even us, who were invited. The idea of watching over Peewee had not crossed my mind.

Bill and Bob and Peewee went fishing. My daughter was away at camp. She wrote: I love you more than my cabinmates love their mothers. I need four dollars for a T-shirt, please send it fast.

Stormy–this was Bob's wife–took me on a tour, tromping around and checking every cabin, though there were all the same. She showed me places in the woods that were good for mushrooms in the spring, and a creek were Peewee could wade when it was hot. She made eggplant sandwiches on sprouted wheat bread, and a drink of orange juice and boiled water. Her father had served time for major crimes. She looked harmless, wearing an Indian gauze skirt, layered for warmth over white cotton long johns that were gray-dirty at the neck and wrists. She was tiny. She spoke in a whispery voice that made me think of Jackie Kennedy when she did that television tour of the White House.

Bob rescued me, Stormy said as we stepped out from a cabin into the murky light. She was smiling. Later Bob bled to death on the floor, because she ran off and left him when the shooting stopped. There wasn't a single vital organ hit, but Bob died. Rescued me from the street, she added, where I never should have gone.

When my daughter was four, a circular welt appeared on the outside of her left ankle. Her teacher at nursery school said she could not come back to class until we saw a doctor, in case it was ringworm. It was something more exotic and acceptable, granuloma annulare. It grew and grew that year, until the soft pink string of flesh was wound up her leg halfway to her knee, and on her foot down to the edge where the toes stick out. It was nothing, it was an immunological aberration that signaled nothing fearful, and it went away without treatment in another year. During that year, I would look at it and think–I would make myself think, like someone fresh from a cognitive behavior session–it's only an overgrown bump. Only granuloma annulare, and not on her hands or face, be glad of that. It could be so much worse, I recited to myself, like I used to say, Jesus, Mary, Joseph, as a Catholic child, praying for indulgence, for forgiveness, for delivery from Purgatory and fear, loss, grief.

When my daughter was fifteen, I picked her up at school one day. She was crying hard. A girl from her World Geography class had written her name in a toilet stall, she said, something ugly. I made her wait in the car. I could not find anything, so I told her it had been cleaned up. I told her not to worry. She wasn't sleeping through the night anymore, she didn't eat, her stomach hurt, she thought kids talked behind her back and teachers were unfair. She spent hours in absolute silence. I started sleeping in her narrow bed with her. So I would wake up when she did, so I could hold her if she wanted. But one night she rose without disturbing me, and ran a bath. I woke when I heard the water running out of the tub. I looked up, and in the moonlight I saw her standing in the doorway to the room where I lay in her bed. She was naked and wet. I thought: she must be cold. When she saw me looking at her, she said there wasn't a towel. It was the saddest thing I'd ever heard her say. She sat down on the floor, dripping water, and I could not lift her, and she would not stand, and she did not speak, and after all the years when I had been so afraid for myself, waiting for my mother to show up from inside me, I felt terror and anger that it was my daughter instead. If this can happen, I thought, then anything can.

I don't read the paper. I watch the news on public television, where there have to be larger issues to merit time on the air. Elections, executions. Earthquakes, wars. I work with a woman whose daughter died horribly; I love her, but I wish I could forget. I don't watch violent movies. But I know what's out there. At night I have wakened and felt a presence in the room. It's okay, I want to say, though I am trembling. Stay here, I can take it. In the morning, I feel so foolish, to have assumed there is only one of whatever it is, and that I can tell it what to do.

"Call me from the airport," I told my daughter when she went away to school. "Lock your bedroom at night." When we visited colleges, I interviewed security directors, but of course in the end she chose. She chose for the funkiness of the studios, the sense of having been courted best, the energy and promise and competition. I didn't want it to be New York.

She lived for a while in New Jersey, in a complex of apartments that seemed safe. The wind made a whistle against her window all the time, never ceasing. At night she could see the lights of the Empire State Building. It was a dark walk to the grocery store, across a weedy vacant lot. She lost weight, and called me at all hours. In February I went to see her, maybe to bring her home. Instead, she moved. Now she lives in a women's residence, facing Gramercy Park. The sounds through her windows are the sounds of a pleasant city neighborhood. She can walk to the studios. It's safe enough, she says. Where is anybody safe?

The woman I work with is graceful, like a dancer, with a gorgeous mane of salt and pepper hair. My daughter was six when this woman's daughter died. For the next ten years there was never a moment when I did not know where my daughter was. I was so careful. I would not let her cross the main street of our town alone until she was nine. She always had to call when she reached the place she was going. The only time I didn't think, I left her pink bicycle on the porch overnight, and in the morning it was gone. I felt stupid. From the porch, while we slept inside.

Nobody said, Why Bob? Did that mean there was some logic to it, something about it that made sense? Isn't that what novelists strive for, meaning and structure? Isn't what they write fiction? His murder was not random. It wasn't for a good reason, either. He did not ask for it. Nobody said: How could this have happened? His mother may have, but I didn't hear. I didn't see her until quite some time after, when she had absorbed it. It had made her heavier, and slow, and in time she learned she had cancer. When I saw her, we did not talk about the disease, but we did talk a little about Bob. What I don't understand, she said, is how she could have left him. She said, Stormy could have saved him.

How could I tell her that I wondered those same things, and that, from my distance, I felt myself inventing answers? How could I make her understand that pain is loamy soil for a writer? That I had already named them, characters now: Buddy, Luna, and Punam.

When Bill's mother was visiting, when we talked about Bob, that was the very day I bought our lot. It is in the next town over from where we were living then. I had gone with my daughter to get the mail, and I didn't know how I would get through the rest of the day. I didn't know what else I could say, so I said to my daughter, let's take a ride. I asked an agent to show me the cheapest lots. He wouldn't go out with us, but he gave me three addresses, and at the second one, there were blackberry bushes and a tiny creek. To the east, near, were low brown hills, looking like chamois in the summer light. I knew that later the hills would look blue, and at another time green, and in winter there would be snow scattered across them. I went home and got everybody to drive back with me, and we bought the lot, just like that. Bill's mother lent us part of the money. We were all excited, agitated, like when a mare has had her foal. I had changed the subject entirely.

The weeks my daughter was in the hospital are her secret. I know that she, like my mother, kept a journal. Whatever secrets were my mother's frightened my dad, and he burned them the day she died. My daughter carries hers with her, even now, parkside. I don't think she means to hide from me, exactly, but I don't know what to ask. "I felt safe there," she told me once, saying it wasn't so bad. "The other kids were interesting." One day she showed me a line in her journal: I feel safe in my mother's kitchen. But if she stays here, we both know, she will never find out who she is. And I like her room, for my own purposes; the light is nice there, too. I lie on her bed for hours and wait to know how a scene will go, what a character will do, how much I will say. I have stopped feeling anxious about that. I don't worry about writer's block, it is too singular a fear. I worry that I won't have enough time, and that I'll never be able to find a form for what I know, what I want to leave. I worry that readers used to soundbites and blips won't have the patience for me. I worry that they won't love my characters and forgive them for being afraid.

I think of my daughter on one of the first days after she came home from the hospital. She sits in the garden, the grapevines at her back, plaiting a bracelet of floss. The vines have found the twine strung between two stakes while we were building. Not hardy, the vines curl onto the twine and hold. Grape clusters the size of thumbs frame her head like flowers.

In the kitchen I am slicing carrots and leeks for soup. In the yard across the trickling ditch, a crow caws. In the kitchen I hear it and wish it dead. I watch my daughter. She lies back in the chair, her arms along her sides, the threads of her unfinished bracelet lumped on her belly rise. The crow flaps and calls. I think: I'll kill it with the soup. I see soup on the crow's head, the spill of leeks across mown grass. I'll drown it, I think. I'll make clear soup instead.

I want to tell her that I'm sorry. I'm so sorry. What you've been through, maybe it's the price of your sensibility. Or something you got from me. I did not know how to keep it from you.

One day in the late summer, before she went away to school, I came upon her in the kitchen, sketching the cat. She was using Conté crayon and a large pad of newsprint, making quick contour drawings that seemed to appear on the page almost without effort. The cat was enjoying the sun, moving her body in a playful dance with the motes in a shaft of light that struck my desk. When the cat finally settled and closed her eyes, my daughter let the crayon fall onto the desk. I was standing a few feet away, behind her, admiring the way her hair brushed her shoulders. "Jess," I said softly. She was looking past the cat, into the brilliant light. She was turned away from me. I didn't think she could see anything out there, looking straight into the light.

Right after we moved into our house, we read that Stormy's father had been sent to prison again. He had killed an old man for a little money. Not long after that, Bob's murderer was released from his short term on a prison farm. No one had seen Stormy since the day Bob was shot, except a man who gave her a ride, who said she had a bandage on her arm and had said it was from an accident, and not serious. I used to think she had died. I dreamed she walked into the ocean above Gold Beach, with Peewee. But she showed up at Bill's mother's house one day a year or so ago, with a boyfriend, and the boy. She needed money. She wanted Bill's mother to fix it with Social Security for her, and when Bill's mother said it was too late, too much time had gone by, Stormy got into the truck and drove away.

I write Bill's mother every month or so. I work in a bookstore, and I send her books. She writes about the weather, and her friends who have died. It has been two years since her radiation treatments, and the tests say she is cancer-free. I write back to say, "Thank God," and "It's only right." I don't tell her any of the stories Bill has told me, the ones about pranks and dangerous games. I might, though, if she lives to be very old. I think she could stand it, then.

Des Moines, Iowa, 1992

SANDRA SCOFIELD is the author of six novels, including *Beyond Deserving,* which was a National Book Award finalist. She is also a book reviewer and works occasionally in her local bookstore in Oregon. Her book *A Chance to See Egypt* will be published this winter.

Interview

John Updike

What made you decide to be a writer?

My mother wanted to be a writer, and from earliest childhood on I saw her at the typewriter; and though my main passion as a child was drawing, I suppose the idea of being a writer was planted in my head.

Which writers did you first admire? Was their work an influence on your early writing?

Of course, everything you read of any merit at all in some way contributes to your knowledge of how to write, but my first literary passion was James Thurber. He showed me an American voice and a willingness to be funny. I think I first became aware of his work when I was around eleven, and I actually would save up pennies to go and buy the new Thurber; he was my idol until about the age of eighteen or nineteen. I wrote him a fan letter when I was twelve and he sent me a drawing, which I've carried with me, framed, everywhere I've gone since. In college there were Shakespeare and Dostoevsky, to name two, and the short stories of J. D. Salinger really opened my eyes as to how you can weave fiction out of a set of events that seem almost unconnected, or very lightly connected.

Directly out of college, in my attempt to continue my education, I began to read Proust in an English translation by Scott Moncrieff, and the length of those sentences, and the qualities of the perceptions he was searching for, the expansive, delicious lunges into philosophy, all seemed very magical to me. At about the same period I also began to read an English novelist called Henry Green, who is semi-forgotten but for me is really a master of the voice of fiction. *Rabbit Is Rich* is a long way from those years, but the pick-and-roll of it, the quickness of it, was written with Green's touch in mind. And, of course, behind all those interior monologues stands *Ulysses*; the interior monologues of both Molly and Leopold Bloom were for me a very liberating, very exciting new way to touch the texture of human experience. But Joyce is in the air you breathe, whereas Proust and Green and Salinger stick in my mind as really having moved me a step up, as it were, toward knowing how to handle my own material.

You once said that, in your novel *Rabbit, Run,* you were interested in dramatizing a kind of scared, dodgy approach to life.

I suppose I could observe, looking around me at American society in 1959, a number of scared and dodgy men–and I felt a certain fright and dodginess within myself. This kind of man who won't hold still, who won't make a commitment, who won't quite pull his load in society, became Harry Angstrom. I imagined him as a former basketball player. As a high school student I saw a lot of basketball and even played a certain amount myself, so the grandeur of being a high-school basketball star was very much on my mind as an observed fact of American life. You have this athletic ability, this tallness, this feeling of having been in some ways a marvelous human being up to the age of eighteen, and then everything afterward running downhill. In that way he accumulated characteristics–even his nickname, Rabbit. Rabbits are dodgy, rabbits are sexy, rabbits are nervous, rabbits like grass and vegetables. I had an image of him that was fairly accessible, and his neural responses, his conversational responses, always seemed to come very readily to me, maybe because they were in many ways like my own.

In *Rabbit Is Rich,* you have chosen an unusual point of view, that of the father, to tell the story of a conflict between a father and his son.

I suppose it's fairly unusual. Most novels are told from the young man's point of view, and are written by authors who probably were that young man not too many years before, so you don't get a very empathetic view towards many fathers. You think of Kafka's father, how he dominates and haunts the Kakfa fiction, but you never really get much of a sense of how the father felt about young Franz.

The father-and-son conflict in *Rabbit Is Rich* just sort of flowed naturally out of Harry's aging. He's better with smaller children than with bigger ones. I think with bigger children you need a certain set of principles, something to hang a disciplinary system on, and he doesn't have that system. So with the twenty-two- or twenty-three-year-old Nelson, Harry is fairly worthless; he just dimly at moments feels sorry for him, but is jealous of his girlfriend, is jealous of his youth, imagines that he enjoys a kind of freedom that he, Harry, never had, and the rest of it. But maybe by Nelson's age a normal boy shouldn't be there in the house with his father. Maybe parenthood has a certain season and curve, and Harry has run his curve of fatherhood and feels deep down that he shouldn't have to mess anymore with this child of his. In a way, the position of the father in this conflict is more interesting since it's more ambivalent. There is love along with real animosity. The father is both the rival and the protector.

You seem particularly interested in inherited traits.

My mother, and her father also, were much interested in family resemblances, and maybe that's what planted this particular theme in my head. One of the things I was trying to show was the power of genes. That is, Nelson is in many ways his father's son, but he is also his mother's son, and Harry is very aware of that, too. He looks at Nelson's hands and sees those little Springer hands. Nelson has the misfortune of being the short son of a tall father. The novel, in a way, is a study of inheritance.

By and large, it's not something you find much in novels, do you? Some of Anne Tyler's books treat families as entities as well as collections of individuals–*Searching for Caleb,* for instance. For the younger writers now the nuclear family has become really nuclear. It's you and Mom and your siblings and maybe Dad, although often he's absent, and you get the feeling of a very narrow focus as far as your own identity goes; whereas in the traditional, stable, small-town setting that I grew up in, you were very aware of your ancestors going back at least to the great-grandfather's generation –and even further, I suppose, if you were an aristocrat.

Does the structure of *Rabbit Is Rich* reflect the action in the novel?

Structurally the novel hinges on the introduction of strangers into the household. Nelson comes home and brings Melanie, disturbing the little social order there; but then Melanie turns out to be just the precursor of Pru, and her introduction creates a whole new order.

The action of the book coincides with Pru's pregnancy; that is, all these quarrels and events and conversations are as it were engraved upon the surface of her swelling belly. The book is about the arrival of yet another Angstrom–the little granddaughter who is finally going to compensate for the death of Harry's daughter twenty years before. Harry is becoming a grandfather, whether he knows it or not, throughout the book. It's a step up, out of the middle range of human experience, into the endgame. When you become a grandparent you're usually the next to go; there's nothing beyond grandparenthood but death, as he senses in the end of the novel.

It's a funny thing; in planning the book, and making this one of the central actions, I kind of imagined I would have become a grandfather by that point. But although I had four children, none of them had produced a grandchild, so I had to make it all up. Now I am a grandfather of five, but all boys, and none as old as Judy.

How do you find it compares to your fictionalized version of grandparenthood?
There's imagination and there's reality, and they're not the same. They're not even in the same ballpark, in a funny way. Although you borrow constantly from real life, in the end what the reader wants, and what you should try to provide, is experience stripped of confusion. Life comes to us full of clutter; every moment is, in a sense, overloaded, and in fiction you try, without totally abandoning that sensation of overload, to hew out entities which have shape and flow.

So it might have been less help than you would think to have been a grandparent then. Indeed, it was a help not to have had any of the experiences in this book, really; it is purer that way. Harry and I began on the same piece of turf and have much of the same basic equipment as other American Protestant white men, but beyond that we diverged. And yet, if I may say so, for me he continued to live. Each book seems easier when it's over with than it did at the time, but there is a kind of ease that I associate with the books about Rabbit. Under the title of *Rabbit Is Rich* there seemed to be a luxuriance; the details were abundant in coming, and I almost had to stop the book forcibly, or it would have gone on forever.

Did *Rabbit Is Rich* mark a certain point in your writing career?
It did some nice things for me. After a long period of prizelessness, winning the National Book Award and the other major fiction prizes of the year felt like an enhancement of my position as an American writer. I felt that not only was I given a prize, but that a prize was given to the idea of trying to write a novel about a more-or-less average person

in a more-or-less average household. That vindicated one of my articles of faith since my beginnings as a writer: that mundane daily life in peacetime is interesting enough to serve as the stuff of fiction.

Beverly Farms, Massachusetts, 1994

JOHN UPDIKE is the author of seventeen novels, along with twenty-some other titles, including six collections of poetry. He received the National Book Award for fiction for *The Centaur* and *Rabbit Is Rich,* and is a six-time finalist for the award. His latest novel, *In the Beauty of the Lilies,* will be published in March. Since 1954, Mr. Updike has been a frequent contributor (of short stories, book reviews, and poems) to *The New Yorker.*

American Academy of Arts and Letters

THE FLAMING
ALL ARTS ARE
ONE ALL BRANCHES
ON

Writers at the Century's Turn

R. W. B. Lewis

Gertrude Stein liked to say that America entered the twentieth century ahead of the rest of the world. In 1933, in *The Autobiography of Alice B. Toklas*, she put it more strongly—that America had actually created the new century:

> America [is] the oldest country in the world, because by the civil war and the commercial conceptions that followed it, America created the twentieth century, a twentieth century life, America, having begun the creation of the twentieth century in the sixties of the nineteenth century, is now the oldest country in the world.

That is of course Stein-language, conveying Stein-paradoxes and surprises in Stein-rhythms; but there is a good deal of truth in the large contention—that "commercial conceptions" in the later nineteenth century, coming out of Civil War upheavals and the resulting economic expansion, effectively determined that cultural atmosphere of the age. F. Scott Fitzgerald, writing his college friend Edmund Wilson, expressed it more succinctly: "Culture follows money" he wrote in a letter from Europe, notifying Wilson that America was replacing Europe as the center of living culture, and New York replacing London. Ann Douglas, in her recent book *Terrible Honesty,* quotes both Stein and Fitzgerald, and elaborates on them in her study of the modernizing of America. She pays particular attention to the city of New York, which she justifiably considers the great hub and symbol of the modernist energy, especially in the 1920s; and within the Manhattan-scape, she lays emphasis on the extraordinary intermix of black and white writers and artists and musicians and performers and stories and rhythms and languages.

But American writers entered the twentieth century and the age of the modern from a good many different directions, and under different impulsions. As the present century is drawing to a close, it behooves us to inquire about what was happening in the cultural world a hundred years ago, and to the writers within it. What was happening then was much like what is happening now: a series of efforts to determine who we were as cultural beings, and where we seemed to be heading. One such effort was the resplendent White City at the World's Columbian Exposition in Chicago in 1893, a powerful sign of the national culture seeking to come into focus, and doing so with such skill that Henry Adams, an entranced observer, let himself believe that America's cultural day had finally dawned. But there were, in retrospect, some difficulties with that assessment. Daniel Burnham was the chief designer of the White City, and in his own dictum, "the influence of the Exposition will be to inspire a reversion to the pure ideal of the ancients." The ancients were represented by their Renaissance emulators, by a colossal Beaux Arts building based on sixteenth-century Roman, Florentine, and Venetian models–most imposingly in the Brunelleschian Duomo atop Richard Morris Hunt's administration building. For better or worse, the cultural theme being sounded was not really an opening into the new century.

Another strong index of cultural self-awareness, a few years after White City, was the opening to the public on November 1, 1997, of the new Library of Congress building in Washington. John Adams had been the one to authorize a Library of Congress in 1800, with the first books arriving from England the next year. Many decades later, a separate building for the enormously expanded Library was approved; and the vast Italian Renaissance building was ready for use. America, it was said in a contemporary guidebook "is justly proud of this gorgeous and palatial monument to its National sympathy and appreciation of Literature, Science and Art... a fitting example for the great thoughts of generations past, present and to be."

And then, only a matter of months after the opening of the Library of Congress, there began to come into being a cultural assembly that would eventually be known as the American Academy of Arts and Letters. The story of this institution is a mixed one–something that shows a certain readiness to move into the unfamiliar, but also a certain hesitation at moving too rapidly. The story replicates the mixture in the country at large of eagerness and apprehension–for despite the heady Stein-language, America did not all at once and altogether plunge into the new epoch.

The Academy began in fact as an Institute–the Institute of Art, Science and Letters, the offspring of the American Social Science Association, and following discussion among several members of the latter over the fall of 1898. The word *Science* was soon dropped from the title; and the Institute, at its inception, consisted of 150 male individuals–90 in literature, 45 in art, and 15 in music. In 1904, the Institute voted to create from within its own membership a smaller but loftier body to be called the Academy of Arts and Letters.

Surveying that membership during the turn-of-the-century years, we discover the comfortably established seated alongside the cautiously innovative. Walt Whitman (who died half a dozen years before the Institute was born) had spoken in despair, in the later 1880s, about the quality of the literati visible on the

American horizon: nothing but "accomplished good-natured persons," he said, performing decorously in polite society, and, as he put it, very knowledgeable about whether the sherry should come before or follow the stewed eels on a dinner menu; "but for real crises, great needs and pulls, moral or physical, they might as well never have been born."

There were a number of such socially knowing and good-natured folk among the charter members of the Institute, not least among the writers. There were of course some literary professors and propounders who, like Charles Eliot Norton, recoiled in horror from the American cultural panorama, with its impending vulgarities, and sought solace from the turmoil amid the orderly attractions of the Middle Ages. But there were also some practicing writers who were possessed of what Lionel Trilling called "the opposing self," and which he defined as an "intense and adverse imagination of the culture in which [the self] has its being." It was creative activity of this kind that truly heralded the cultural world to come.

Mark Twain, for example, had an elaborately adverse imagination of his native culture, be it ever so obliquely expressed, whether his imagination focused on the old southern slave society or the new reverence for business and money. Henry James, in his last novels, displayed an awareness–perhaps even greater than he realized–of the violent destructiveness that could lurk behind the well-mannered conduct of the socially adept; and he disclosed as well the doomed disintegrating condition of the society which they represented. William Dean Howells was spurred to active adversity by the pressure of circumstances, specifically by the Haymarket Square riot in Chicago in 1886 and the hideous injustices that followed. Howells, to be sure, was an agreeable kind of social critic, a person given to taking part in protest marches, and, perhaps the same day, showing up at a fashionable tea party. And meanwhile, in his own fictional writings, in his exceedingly influential reviews and articles, and in private words of encouragement, Howells opened the way for realistic fiction–for fiction immersed in and searchingly critical of the historical actualities of the turn-of-the-century day in America. Hamlin Garland (*Main-Travelled Roads*) and Henry Blake Fuller (*The Cliff-Dwellers*) owed a great deal to Howells. Stephen Crane and Frank Norris found in Howells their sole distinguished champion.

Neither Crane nor Norris was a member of the Arts and Letters organization (Garland and Fuller were enrolled at the outset). Stephen Crane's brilliant tales of lyrical realism (*Maggie, George's Mother*) appeared in the 1890s, but Crane died in 1900 at the age of twenty-eight, before institutional recognition of him was possible. Frank Norris also died prematurely, in 1902 at the age of thirty-two, but his forward-looking novels of industrial greed and brutality (*McTeague, The Octopus, The Pit*) could never have won him sufficient votes from the establishment.

Norris bore the stigma, as well, of being a far westerner, having settled at an early age in San Francisco. The Institute had not wholly neglected the regions to the south and west of the eastern seaboard. The Kentuckian John Fox, Jr., (*The Little Shepherd of Kingdom Come*) had been taken in, and so had the Ohioan Edward Eggleston (*The Hoosier Schoolmaster*). But Californians seemed somehow to belong to an inconceivably remote and possibly alien country; and, in the eastern perspective; it should be added that this opinion would hold true among the entrenched easterners for many decades to come.

Jack London may be another writer rendered ineligible by his San Francisco background. But London's powerful fantasy-vision of the taking over of a Socialist band (*The Iron Heel*, 1908), was enough to keep him out of the Academy, even if it endeared him to the anarchist Emma Goldman. Political bias presumably accounts for the exclusion of Upton Sinclair, whose novel *The Jungle* in 1906 displayed a severely adverse imagination of the American social and political order. Sinclair was admitted in 1944, in his sixty-seventh year, and while he was producing the more politically acceptable Lanny Budd novels.

And then there was the midwesterner and tentative easterner Theodore Dreiser, hardly knowable in the 1900s, but emerging gradually as a literary titan. There was talk of electing Dreiser in 1935, but he put a stop to it–out of well-grounded resentment, it seems, that he had not been taken in at least twenty years earlier.

The Department of Art in the 1898 Institute was dominated by the American Impressionists: Childe Hassam, William Merritt Chase, John H. Twachtman, J. Alden Weir, and others. They were Europeanized to an extent, and gentlemanly in exterior manner; but they were genuine painters, with an enlivening appreciation of natural settings. For *younger* painters, however, natural vistas had less appeal than urban scenes as the new century arrived. Jules Prown made the point in his history of American painting up to 1912 that "they wanted to go where the action was, and the action was in the city"; and Prown points to affinities between the young urban artists–Robert Henri, John Sloan, George Luks, and George Bellows–and such contemporary writers as Dreiser and Norris. These, with others, comprised what became know in 1907 as the Ashcan School; and for all the derision heaped upon them, they played a large part in creating the epochal Armory Show in 1913.

Music in America, as of 1900, was much less developed than literature and the arts, and its practitioners acknowledged as much. The distinction among musicologists and composers in this sphere was between adherents of "the historical forms developed by Bach, Handel, Mozart and Beethoven" (I am quoting from John K. Paine, the first professor of music at Harvard), and those who favored the "complicated technics of...Wagner, Liszt" and their associates. (It must be remembered that the works of Charles Ives, the supreme American modernist in music, would not even be performed until the 1940s, though some were in existence as early as 1900.)

It was in the field of music, even so, that the most unmistakably modern note was struck: in an article of 1895 by Antonin

Dvořák, reflecting on his visit to the United States. The composer of the *New World Symphony* expressed the lively hope that a "truly national music" might arise in America, and advanced the proposition that such music "might be derived from the negro melodies and Indian chants." He wrote of "the so-called plantation songs" as "the most stirring and appealing melodies that have yet been found on this side of the water," and (all perceptively) praised their "unusual and subtle harmonies." Within the establishment, however, the national spirit of music in America would have to await the appearance of Aaron Copland well along into the twentieth century.

The makeup of the Institute and Academy of Arts and Letters showed some other noteworthy absences or gaps in the early years. There were no women at all for nearly a decade, despite occasional agitation on their behalf, mainly by Thomas Wentworth Higginson, the stalwart aging social activist whose career had included the command of the first black regiment in the Civil War and the editorial support of Emily Dickinson's poetry. Julia Ward Howe was finally elected in 1907, at the age of eighty-six; she had done conspicuously valuable work in abolition and women's suffrage, but most of the ballots in her favor were endorsing both an old friend and the author of "The Battle Hymn of the Republic." The first woman elected truly and properly as a writer was Edith Wharton, and she not until 1926.

We have no difficulty today in discerning a host of women more than sufficiently accomplished in 1900 to be welcomed in the Arts and Letters organization. There was an array of writers, even if we stay with those who had clearly earned a name and a following, and without regard for those many others who have been brought into view by recent canonical revisions. Harriet Beecher Stowe had died in 1896, and Rose Terry Cooke, the quietly adroit spinner of tales about rustic New England life (*Somebody's Neighbors,* 1881) had died four years before that. But very visible and flourishing in 1900, in addition to Edith Wharton, were Sarah Orne Jewett, whose *The Country of the Pointed Firs* is a classic of American fiction, a case study in the beginnings of a native literary modernism; Mary Wilkins Freeman, who, with Cooke and Jewett, helped advance the short story in America from anecdote to art (*A New England Nun and Other Stories*, 1891); and Kate Chopin of St. Louis and Louisiana, the author of the alarming masterpiece, *The Awakening*, in 1899.

In art, Cecilia Beaux, a bold and original portraitist, known to several of the country's most famous men who sat for her, was available; and Mary Cassatt, the greatest woman artist of the age (though she lived until 1926, Mary Cassatt appears never to have even been mentioned in Arts and Letters discussions). In music, the name that arises is that of Amy Marcy Cheney Beach, a thoroughly professional composer in the romantic tradition.

The possibility of admitting women was at least chatted about in these formative years of the Institute; but no one, so far as can be discovered, ever proposed the nomination of a black person. We should not, however, vaunt ourselves on our late twentieth century enlightenment; and if the presence of minority figures was not sought in the cultural establishments century ago, nor was it anywhere else; nor would it be for sixty or seventy years to come, and then only haltingly.

Ann Douglas, in *Terrible Honesty*, describes a positive explosion of black talent–in some cases, of genius–in the New York of the 1920s, and lists among many others: writers Countee Cullen, Jean Toomer, Langston Hughes, Zora Neale Hurston, and Jessie Fauset; intellectual leaders Alain Locke, James Weldon Johnson, and W.E.B. Du Bois; and musicians and composer-lyricists Eubie Blake, Fats Waller, Louis Armstrong, and Duke Ellington. For Douglas, this extraordinary array of black creativeness and expressiveness is the very sign and seal of the triumph of the modern in twentieth-century American culture. Her argument can lead us to observe that several black writers and artists of achievement were or could have been visible at the century's start. Frederick Douglass had died in 1892; but on the scene and still flourishing were Paul Laurence Dunbar, son of former

Kentucky slaves, the short-lived (1872-1906) author of several volumes of humorous language-twisting poetry (*Oaks and Ivy* among them) that in effect—and once again with the public endorsement of Howells—established black poetry in America. Charles Chesnutt (who died in 1932), produced two books of fiction (*Conjure Woman* and *The Wife of His Youth*), which did the same for black fiction. Just emerging as the new century began was W.E.B. Du Bois; he incarnated a whole segment of American history in this century, but his seminal work *The Souls of Black Folk* came out in 1903, the same year he issued his call for "The Talented Tenth," appealing to the talented 10 percent of the black American community to rise to the grand cultural challenge of their generation and save "the Negro race" in America.

So if America did enter the twentieth century ahead of the rest of the world, the Academy and Institute of Arts and Letters entered the new century in a somewhat gingerly manner. In one respect, the makeup of the Academy suggested a certain alertness to new historical ventures and experiences; and this was exactly an intensifying concern with history itself.

Alexis de Tocqueville, in *Democracy in America* in the 1830s, had said repeatedly that a democratic people would have no interest in history, that in America "no one cares for what occurred before his time," and that democratic art and literature would not examine human beings in historical settings, but would deal rather with "Man himself, taken apart from his country and his age." Tocqueville's predictions held true in part for the literature of the age of Emerson; and some of his pronouncements strike a resonant chord today—especially when one reencounters the persistent historical ignorance or indifference of "the average American," or the persistent tendency toward the dehumanizing abstract by so many of our intellectuals. But sixty years after *Democracy in America,* as the new century awaited, a sophisticated knowledge of history had almost become the mark of the educated man.

Primary among the causes for this remarkable development

must be the colossal event of the Civil War. There is much to be said for Robert Penn Warren's argument in *The Legacy of the Civil War* that for Americans, history—that is, the consciousness of history as something alive and ongoing—was the permanent legacy of the great conflict. And with this thesis, we return to the contention of Gertrude Stein that in a fundamental way the Civil War led to the creation of the twentieth century.

When the Academy of Arts and Letters was carved out of the original Institute in 1904, a number of the very first to be honored could be classified as historians—indeed, as historians of the American experience: Henry Adams; John Hay, the author with John Nicolay of the ten-volume *Abraham Lincoln* in 1891 (as well as a poet, novelist, and journalist); Theodore Roosevelt, who composed his vigorous Parkmanesque four-volume *The Winning of the West* in the late 1890s.

Fiction writers too were exploring the social reality around them, and discovering signs of a society in a moment of great and perhaps tragic transition. Henry James's Densher, wandering through rain-swept Venice in *The Wings of the Dove,* sees in the spectacle an image of the whole of Europe "profaned and bewildered by some reverse of fortune." Howells in novel after novel showed American urban society being critically battered by economic and political forces that dislocated the past without quite establishing the future. Edith Wharton had perhaps the finest sociohistorical intuitions in her literary time: expressed typically in *The House of Mirth* (1905), when Lily Bart walking dispiritedly "through the dreary March twilight" from the New York hat shop where she is now employed to her boardinghouse, makes her way (the image seems to be both Lily's and Wharton's) "through the degradation of a New York street in the last stages of decline from fashion to commerce."

As the new century was ushered in, accordingly, the native artistic attention (and one could cite the historical statuary of Saint-Gaudens as well) was being drawn in to an unprecedented degree toward the country's historical life and even to the historical moment. Something was about to happen.

Among members of the Academy, no one belonged more resolu-tely and imaginatively to the new century and the modern American age than William James. Consider his response to the city of New York when he visited there in 1907. His brother, Henry, had almost been lifted into the twentieth century by the impact upon him of New York a few years earlier. Returning to New York for a lengthy American visit in 1904, Henry found a spectacularly different urban entity. Parts of it appalled him. The city's skyline building, he wrote (not without acuteness), seemed to him "consecrated by no uses save the commercial at any cost"; they were simply "the most piercing notes in the concert of the expensively provisional into which your supreme sense of New York resolves itself." But the great observer and fictional-historian also responded with a rare and even Whitmanian exuberance. As his Washington–Boston Pullman was being transported around the foot of Manhattan on barges, Henry James, looking out at the whole urban display, found in it "the appeal of a particular type of dauntless power... The aspect the power wears then is indescribable; it is the power of the most extravagant of cities, rejoicing as with the voice of morning in its might, its fortune, its unsurpassable conditions, and imparting to every object and element... something of its sharp free accent."

William James came to New York in the winter of 1907 to deliver his lectures on pragmatism at Columbia University, and was altogether captivated by the city. On earlier visits, he had been put off by what he called the "clangor" and "disorder" of the metropolis; now, installed at the midtown Harvard Club, he rejoiced at being, so he put it, "in the center of the cyclone." He "caught the pulse of the machine, took up the rhythm and vibrated *mit,* and found it simply magnificent." Vibrating *mit*—moving in harmony with—his historical and cultural and even technological surroundings could almost serve as a defining phrase for William James. He went up every weekday morning by subway to the Columbia campus and came back that evening, roaring back and forth between the two locations, and exulted to Henry about the "superbly powerful and beautiful" new transportation system (it had opened in 1904). As to the city itself, William's words are an extraordinary reflection of the modern awareness—of the new and forward-bending. Listen to them:

> It is an entirely *new* New York, in soul as well as in body, from the old one which looks like a village in retrospect. The courage, the heaven-scaling audacity of it all, and the *lightness* withal, as if there was nothing that was not easy, and the great pulses and bounds of progress, so many in directions all simultaneous that the coordination is indefinitely future, give a kind of *drumming background* of life that I never felt before.

If the American city, and most especially New York, is the emblem and the scene of American cultural modernism, William James is its first poet.

That lyrical urban consciousness, so to call it, arose on James's part from a unique cast of mind. His younger Harvard colleague George Santayana put it exactly when he wrote in an essay of 1911 that:

> Convictions and ideas came to him...from the subsoil. He had a prophetic sympathy with the dawning sentiments of the age, with the moods of the dumb majority... His way of thinking and feeling represented the true America, and represented in a measure of the whole ultra-modern radical world.

As representative of that "ultra-modern radical world," William James was the philosophic champion of manyness; of variety and alternative and experiment. He would have welcomed the current talk about multiculturalism and multiraciality, while scorning the bigotry and belligerence that often accompanies it.

James reached a kind of peak of new-century and new-world envisioning in his final lecture on pragmatism, where he addresses what he calls an adventurous universe; a universe in which adventure is still possible; and where he describes an openness and possible future not just for individuals but for the entire universe. According to James, at this point pragmatism says that the world can be improved, but only here and there, in bits and pieces: "Our acts, our turning-points, where we seem to ourselves and grow...why may they not be the actual turning-points and growing-places of the world?" He advances a breathtaking hypothesis. Supposing, he says, that the world's author had said to human beings: "I am going to make a world not certain to be saved, a world the perfection of which shall be conditional merely... I offer you the chance of taking part in such a world. Its safety, you see, is unwarranted. It is a real adventure with real danger, yet it may win though... Will you trust the other agents enough to face the risk?"

That remarkable formulation might be described as a kind of democratic metaphysic–the invited participation of the many in the creation of reality itself. It might also be called a frontier metaphysic–and a modernist metaphysic. It certainly expressed an intellectual and rhetorical daring that a few hardy literary and artistic souls, at least, felt inspired by the century's turn.

Lewiston, Maine, 1995

R. W. B. LEWIS was from 1959 to1988 Professor of English and American Studies at Yale University (from 1975, Neil Gray Professor of Rhetoric). Among his many books (three of which have been National Book Award finalists) are *The Poetry of Hart Crane*; *Edith Wharton: A Biography* (which won the Pulitzer Prize); and most recently *The City of Florence*. Professor Lewis's *Robert Penn Warren: The Poems of His Life* will be published next year.

Interview

David McCullough

Do you think of yourself as a writer first, or as a historian? Or are the two inseparable?

I think of myself as a writer who has found in the past an opportunity for self-expression that for many reasons, some of which I'm probably not able to understand myself, appeals to me more than any other. I feel, too, that I'm working in a tradition of writers who for the most part were journalists to begin with, and who have written history and biography for the large general readership: people like Bruce Catton, Barbara Tuchman, Paul Horgan, Wallace Stegner, Robert Caro, Robert Massie, William Manchester, Jean Strouse—there's a long list. We are all trying to write as writers and use the larger past as a way of saying things that we feel strongly.

I'm always drawn to a good story—that's foremost. I'm very much interested in the power of the fundamental narrative of what happened.

When did you first become interested in writing?

It was in college that I began to think seriously about being a writer, though I hardly dared say so. There were others in my class at Yale who talked openly about being writers, and some dressed the part–long scarves, and the like–but I never had the nerve or presumption to say I was going to be a writer. I knew how far I had to go. I knew I'd have to serve an apprenticeship of some kind. I worked first at Time-Life, then for the U.S. Information Agency, and after that for six years at *American Heritage* magazine. I learned a lot, by writing a great deal, but also by working with a number of superb writers and editors –Richard Ketchum and Alvin Josephy in particular.

What inspired your first book, *The Johnstown Flood?*

I had seen some newly acquired photographs at the Library of Congress, amazing pictures taken by a Pittsburgh photographer within a few days of the flood, and when I saw the destruction and horror, I wanted to know more. I had also recently read an interview with Thornton Wilder in one of the *Paris Review* collections–a book I still keep on the shelf beside me–and in there Wilder is asked how he came upon the ideas for his novels and plays. He said he imagined a story he would like to read or a play he would like to see, and if no one had written that story or play, he would write it. And I thought to myself, you've just read two books about the Johnstown Flood that you found unsatisfactory; why don't you attempt to write the book you'd like to read? Since then, my work has tended to center on the creative aspects of civilization, rather than the destructive aspects. To a large extent, my books are about integrity and accomplishment, about people rising to achievement greater than what others expect or maybe even they themselves expect.

What led you to write about Theodore Roosevelt?

After I had finished my book about the Panama Canal, it was as if I'd been working for six years on a great mural. What I wanted to do after that was the reverse, something much smaller in focus, something much more contained in form. It would be as if I were saying, "Come here and look at this miniature." Instead of a great big cast of characters, as in the Panama story, I wanted to take a part of the life of just one person and see what happened.

It's very easy to talk about why one character might make a particularly interesting subject, and I enjoy and indulge in it. But those questions have very little to do with the decision to proceed. The subject reaches out and takes you; it lights the imagination. A kind of love affair with the idea of the book must be there or you can't possibly sustain the work year after year. It feeds the energy and vitality of writing. But I must emphasize you have to have the material to work with. With the Roosevelts, you have a family that wrote thousands of letters and kept diaries that have survived. So there's every chance to get below the surface, which is really the writer's job.

Were you then attracted to biography as a form?

I never intended it to be a biography; I thought of it as a story. In most biographies the main character is seen to grow and change, while the people around him are sort of given to you as fixed entities. But that isn't how life is—everybody is changing and growing and rising or declining. I felt it particularly important to see young Theodore in the context of his family. It's really a book about the growth and change and the influence of six people on one another.

How did this particular narrative take shape?

It's not until I've soaked myself in the material, and in the revelations that come not just from the research but also from the writing, that I begin to sense what's at the root of it all. *Mornings on Horseback* is the story of the metamorphosis of a frightened, peculiar, sick little boy into the man who will become the symbol of American vitality and virility and purpose at the start of the new century. It's about liberation. The family saves his life, with boundless affection and support, but he can't be himself until he gets away from the family. His asthma is part of a handicapped, constrictive, sympathy-garnering childhood he must outgrow. When he leaves home, he becomes Theodore Roosevelt.

This was the first book where I felt I had an opportunity to be more the writer and less the historian. The fact that the book doesn't begin with birth or end in death gives it freedom at each end. And it's in many ways the most intimate of my books; I could expand on the character because I didn't have to do the whole life.

What are the pleasures and challenges for you in writing about one person?

The chief pleasure is you get to keep company with a fascinating and protean character, if you choose someone like Theodore Roosevelt. It's a privilege, as well as a tonic. The hardest thing is to convey that events and decisions were all happening in an atmosphere of freedom, and not as if all on a preordained track. Nothing ever had to happen as it did. Again, this is something—a *writing* problem—that Thornton Wilder talked about. You have to build your capacity for empathy when writing about people from the past—to put yourself in their shoes and their time, so you can know what it was like to have been alive in their place, alive in their time. You must avoid the hubris that comes from hindsight.

Can you explain how the past continues to pull on your imagination?

Most people think of history as old dead stuff, and who can blame them? It's so often presented that way, like bad-tasting medicine that supposedly is good for you. History is about life—about people, people, people—and the writing must bring these people and their times to life. The story of our country is so strong, so compelling, so very important. I want to share the wealth.

West Tisbury, Massachusetts, 1993

DAVID McCULLOUGH is the author of *The Path Between the Seas*, and *Mornings on Horseback*, which both won National Book Awards. His most recent biography, *Truman*, was a finalist for the award. In 1995, he received the National Book Foundation Medal for Distinguished Contribution to American Letters.

Washington Irving High School, New York City

Dogma

John Casey

The most common thing people ask me about writing is "Where on earth do you get those ideas?" Perhaps there'll be time for that question a little later.

The second most common thing people ask is "Can you teach someone to write?"

I have two answers.

The first is "No"...but if someone is talented to begin with, I can save her a lot of time.

The second answer is also "No"...I can't teach someone to write, but I can sometimes teach someone to rewrite.

For a long time I taught the way I'd been taught. I'd been in classes taught by Peter Taylor, Kurt Vonnegut, Vance Bourjaily, José Donoso, and what they did–after you turned in a story–was to tell you what they thought you'd done. Basically they'd say "Here is what all those marks on the pages meant to me."

And then I could figure out if that's what I'd wanted to do...or if there was now something else I could do that looked better.

This holding the mirror up is a good way to be helpful to a beginning writer. Writing a story or a novel is like finding your way around a strange room in the dark. When you get through the first draft you think the light will go on. But it often doesn't. At first you need a reader you can trust to tell you what you've done...and that there is or isn't hope for this particular effort.

I think this process is useful because the majority of good beginning writers are at first less in love with structure or pattern and more in love with the *words* in a foolish but sweet way.

I don't think people should skip this sweet foolishness. There is this to be said for it: you are falling deeply in love with language; you are, at last, learning your own language. If the sweetness outweighs the foolishness, if the genuine outweighs the synthetic, if the verbal inventiveness and precision outweigh the clichés of plot and callow characterization, it's a helpful stage. It may be as good for the future as plowing under a field full of oats.

When Katherine Anne Porter taught at the University of Virginia, her method was to sit the student writer down and read his story to him aloud. That's all there was to it, or so I've heard tell. I've also heard that one student, before his story was half read, broke down and ran.

I'm sympathetic. Long ago a kind editor at a Boston publishing house took an interest in my earliest novel. Over lunch he told me, "You have talent, dear boy." I felt for an instant like one of those saints in Italian paintings on whom a beam of divine light falls. He then said, "Of course, some of this writing is... embarrassing." "Oh yeah," I said, "Like what?" (Sometimes you just can't help leading with your chin.)

He opened the manuscript and read aloud.

After a bit I said, "Ahh." Or maybe it was "Arrrgh."

He advised me to plow it all under. I did.

Three years later I salvaged a part of a chapter, turned it inside out, and used it in a story, the first piece I sold. (Moral: plow under, but save a copy just in case.)

But the sophomore, the wise fool, the sweet fool, has to be done away with sooner or later. So what comes next?

From the writer's point of view it seems like more of the same: the inspiration, the rise of hope, the realization, on one's own now, that some part of the piece has failed. You've had your hand held, someone has held up a mirror, but now it's time for sterner stuff. Dogma.

Is dogma helpful? Let us hear some:

- "Write for yourself"–*J. D. Salinger,* or at least one of the Glass boys.
- "Write about what you know"–*Everybody* says that.
- "Above all, I want to make you see"–*Joseph Conrad.*
- "You must tell your story in the fewest words possible" –*Sean O'Faolain.*
- "A short story must have a single mood and every sentence must build towards it"–*Edgar Allen Poe.*
- "Tell the truth"–Everyone again.
- "Stalk the many-headed beast–be a reporter"–*Tom Wolfe.*
- "Conventional narrative bores me; you must experiment" –*Robert Coover.*
- "Culture is local"–*William Carlos Williams.*

There are many other dicta, but these are all at the core. They are also ones I've been told, have told myself, and have told others; frequently they were just what the doctor ordered.

Salinger's "Write for yourself." Yes, there is something wonderful about a writer who has her own voice. And there is something horrible about the sound of an imitated voice. There are writers whose works you can pick up and the particular hum of the prose is immediately recognizable; there is an intimacy your inner ear recognizes even before the rest of your brain approves. This intimacy is not necessarily gentle or nice, but I'm pretty sure that the only way to achieve it is in communion with yourself, a communion that is in some way innocent, however fierce or forgiving.

Of course, the dictum applies to subject matter as well as tone or style. It can be a good prescription for the stylishly voiced but timid. Find the subject that leaves you mute, then tell it.

BUT. If you were to take this dictum as your only course and not a course correction, you could end up on the rocks.

Arthur Koestler, in the second chapter of his autobiography *Arrow in the Blue,* justifies himself and apologizes for autobiography in general. Among his warnings, the chief is against nostalgia.

Twenty years ago I covered a bass-fishing tournament for *True* magazine. The winner of the tournament was a laconic fishing guide from Arkansas. I spent a day with him picking up tips on how to catch fish–the conditions of structure, season, sun, etc. I asked him at least if there were things to watch out for in all this finding the right spot to fish.

"Nostalgia," he said.

I figured out what he meant. I'd spent hours plugging away at a stretch of water where I remembered with great pleasure catching a beauty. But if the fish aren't there now, all you catch is nostalgia. Moonbeams of your peculiar unrelatable memory.

BUT. There's another *but.* Kurt Vonnegut used to say to his class at Iowa, "You've got to be a good date for the reader." The rest of the metaphor of courtship could be inferred. Query: Can you bring flowers and write for yourself? Can you wear perfume and write for yourself? As long as it's still you.

But surely you have some friends to whom you would never ever say–just before they set out for a blind date–"Oh, just be yourself."

There is a falsity or pandering one must rid oneself of, but there is often a sincere but boring side too. If I were to go on a blind date, I'm sure that my wife, four daughters, and three sisters would all call out "For God's sake, don't talk about rowing!"

"Be a good date" can let you be a mere entertainer.

"Write for yourself" can let you be a nostalgic bore.

But in the sense that "write for yourself" is "know yourself," "find your own demon, your own angel," it is the first commandment of useful dogma.

"Write about what you know." An example of this as good advice:

I had two students who were writing costume drama. One was writing about Mayan warriors–sacrifice, sex, and slaughter. The other about gentlewomen in Alabama in hoop skirts. Both went on and on. I finally said to each, "Stop."

The woman who'd been going on about hoop skirts, said, "What shall I write about then?"

"Talk to me a bit, tell me what you know."

She said, "I see you're looking at my knee..."–This was back in the first round of miniskirts. She went on, "See how it doesn't quite fit? It's going to make me lame unless I have an operation but I have had a phobia of hospitals ever since I was strapped to a gurney when I was little. It was a Labor Day weekend and the room was full of people screaming, I was there for hours, days, I can still hear them whenever I smell that hospital smell...whenever I smell that hospital smell I get migraines so bad I can't see, literally, can't see..."

I said, "Come back in two weeks with seven pages about your knee."

She wrote a five-page piece called "Patella" that was riveting. It was, in the apt phrase of my first wife, "hysterically calm." It won the $500 prize for the best short story at the University of Virginia.

So I told the man the same thing. Write a five-page story about something closer to you than Mayan slaughter. He came back with a wonderfully condensed piece about a man sitting at mass (about a quarter of the writing was simply the words of the mass). There was a woman next to him. Her sleeve brushed his sleeve. He concentrated on prayer. Her shoulder brushed his. Was she doing it on purpose? Was she sick? Fainting?

They stood for the Gospel. He wouldn't let himself look at her. He only saw the hem of her raincoat when they sat down. He listened to her breathe. He tried to concentrate on the sermon.

I don't remember how it ended. It was abrupt I think. *Ite, missa est.* Go, the mass is ended. He (the character) was still caught in uncertainty; he'd half resisted the temptation, half succumbed...if the temptation was really there. He was freed by the fact that he could never possibly recognize her, never find out what she'd meant. Perhaps there was some regret.

I thought how much more full of conjured sensuality, of tension, of a real psyche and spirit this piece was than all the hundred and fifty pages of exotic Mayan sex and slaughter.

"Write about what you know"...could there be any *buts*? Two occur to me. Suppose Tolstoy had decided to end *The Death of Ivan Ilych* before Ivan Ilych is dying and has a vision–because Tolstoy didn't really know what dying is. One answer is that Tolstoy imagined it so vividly that he *did* know. Flaubert imagined the death agony of Madame Bovary so intensely that he vomited. Perhaps the best version of this dogma for some people is "Write about what you know, but move into that rich intertidal zone between the dry beach of what you know and the sea of what you don't."

Kipling wrote wonderful stories about the Indian Army. He'd hung out with them when he was a reporter in India. Later, when he'd become famous and was living in England, the Royal Navy made him an honorary officer and asked him to come on training cruises. He got royal tours of the ships–the engine room, the bridge, the officer's ward room, etc. Kipling was an inquisitive man and a quick study. He used his navy material, but the navy stories are lifeless. They are filled with navy lingo and detail, but they don't live. What is the moral of this experience? It may be that if you acquire technical knowledge quickly, without the slower sense of the emotional forces carried by these *things* in a communal life, you will prattle. Even if you are Kipling. Perhaps the qualifying dictum is: he who learns a little soon repeats it. Kipling had some of his best work still ahead of him from "They" (1904) "The Wish House" (1924) and on into the thirties. I love stories about writers with rich autumnal years.

Conrad's "Above all, I want to make you see" is a wonderful motto. Fiction often fails because it isn't visible enough. I see my own early bad writing repeated year after year by otherwise gifted young writers because they want to get right to the metaphysics. But when they or I get to what things look like–not just picturesque landscapes but people's expressions, light on water, the way a worker works–things perk up.

Hemingway had a similar motto something like Conrad's. It's more or less this: write about what people did, what people said, and what the weather was like. Cyril Connolly in his wonderful and odd book *The Unquiet Grave* gives Hemingway his due for having succeeded in awakening the readers' senses.

But the real wonder of fiction is that it not only appeals to the senses–it makes all of your shadow senses receive the world of the story–but also at its very best it gives us a sixth sense: a sense of the invisible forces that make people more than the sum of their five senses. Conrad, though he is the author of the motto, certainly conjured the invisible as well as the visible. As writers, you do finally have to conjure, whether by implication or direct statement, invisible forces as specifically as you have conjured a bullfight, a bank robbery, a kiss. Consider the end of *The Great Gatsby.* The end of *The Sun Also Rises.* All of *Nostromo.*

So perhaps we can amend Conrad and say "First of all, I want to make you see." If you can do that then you can go on, then you have earned the right to the invisible.

"You must tell your story in the fewest words possible." The book in which Sean O'Faolain says this, *The Short Story,* is one of the few useful works on the subject. It is one half anthology, one half commentary.

I can't explain why shortness is a good thing. I can only think of how many gallons of maple sap it takes to make one gallon of maple syrup–forty. Maple sap tastes like water–very good water, but water. Maple syrup is a miracle.

Sean O'Faolain doesn't mean you have to send a telegram. Nor does he mean that you must tell simple stories that begin with the beginning, go through a middle and stop at the end. Supreme examples of rigorous cutting and condensations are Isaac Babel's *Red Cavalry* and Muriel Spark's *The Girls of Slender Means.*

I believed this dictum even before I read it. It was in the babbling gossip of the air. The first story I sold was one I con densed. For ten evenings I more or less copied the handwritten pages of the third and what I thought was the final draft onto new pages, and, at the end of each evening, I would count with satisfaction, "There: four pages into three." Next time–"There: six pages into four and a half."

Reading aloud helps. You can feel the places where the density isn't what it should be. Reading aloud to prepare a piece for reading aloud in public helps even more. You tend to ask yourself, "Do all those people need to know all of this?"

BUT. Even here there is a *but.* Sean O'Faolain tries to demonstrate how Henry James's long story "The Real Thing" can be cut. He puts brackets around the unnecessary parts. He was brave enough to pick a story by a master. It's a very close call whether he has improved the James story. My students have split about fifty-fifty on this question.

My own further experience is odd. My first published novel, *An American Romance,* was 604 pages in typescript when I sent it to my agent and to my editor. They both said, "Way too long. Make it shorter."

I worked for six or seven months. There were 100 pages on the floor of my workroom when I finished. I did write a few little additions. I typed it up again. It came to 640 pages. What the hell. I sent it in.

My agent and my editor wrote back independently of each other, "Good. It's much shorter."

An Italian fencing master I once knew used to ask his students, "How does the frog catch the fly? Because he is quickest? No! Because he has *tempo*!"

Tempo, timing, pace, rhythm. The shortest distance between two points is a frog's tongue. Thank you, maestro.

"A short story must have a single mood..." Poe went on to say that every sentence must contribute to it. He wrote this in a review of Hawthorne's stories, saying that Hawthorne brilliantly fulfilled this requirement of unity and coherence. So do a lot of Poe stories. The dictum is a terrific idea, one I'd guess he came to from his reading and writing lyric poetry. It is a short-story writer's alternative to the suggestions about unity made by Aristotle for tragedy, which show up sometimes as rigid law (one main character, one day, one place). If you haven't already read Aristotle's *Poetics,* it's worth the two or three times you have to read it to sift out the message. The difficulty is in part due to a patched-together text, so some scholarly apparatus, available in most modern paperbacks, is helpful. Aristotle's mood is much sweeter than his descendants'. It is something like this: You playwrights have given me such great pleasure, I hope you don't mind if I make a few suggestions about how you can increase my tragic pleasure.

This is a critical mood I wouldn't mind seeing make a comeback.

Both Poe and Aristotle are trying to be helpful in this quest for unity. But what's so hot about unity?

I can't explain unity any more than I did brevity. In *The Biology of Art,* Desmond Morris writes that certain apes and a few monkeys produce paintings that show an instinctual urge toward both symmetry and unity. It is a fascinating book with lots of beautiful pictures, particularly some by chimpanzees (Picasso owned a picture by Congo, the star chimp artist); I

I also like the delicate spirals turned out by the capuchin monkeys, and some of the work by Sophie, a gorilla who would only paint when she was separated from her mate.

Kurt Vonnegut has a nice sentence about yearning for unity–and brevity too–in *Slaughterhouse Five.* The beings of Tralfamadore, a distant planet, have novels; each is a single dot that fits on your fingertip and zaps you with the essence of the novel.

My own daydream of unity could have been the Parthenon, the Pantheon, or a well-wrought urn, but at the particular right moment I happened to see a catboat on her cradle. Her lines defined her perfectly, yet didn't seem to be limits. Every line curved toward another, but didn't end when it met the other. All the lines seemed endless continuations of each other, an endless continuation of the whole. She was a single idea that looked enormous in a neat way, but also as if you could pick her up in the palm of your hand.

Virginia Woolf describes a character in *The Years* having a physical experience of architecture. Considering a building, she (the character) feels weights move inside her until (I may be making up this part) on their own they find the balance the building has. It is possible to read some buildings in that way: standing in the center or sensing their center from outside, you feel their balance so enormously but so wholly that you imagine you could extend your fingertips to every part.

Are there stories or novels like that? One of the pleasures of the days following reading *Pride and Prejudice, Moby Dick, Madame Bovary*–and many others–or stories like Gogol's "Overcoat," its descendant, Frank O'Connor's "Guests of the Nation," Eudora Welty's "Why I Live at the P.O.," Faulkner's "Barn Burning," Flannery O'Connor's "A Good Man Is Hard to Find" is that sensation of feeling the lines moving out and around and back through the whole.

Could there be any *buts* about the unity that Poe or Aristotle, each in his own way, wish for us?

There *are* buildings like the one in Virginia Woolf's *The Years,* like the Pantheon and its descendants by Palladio and Jefferson. Yet there are others like that in which the prince in Lampedusa's *The Leopard* lives. As I remember it, he thinks that it would be boring to live in a house in which you knew all the rooms. I imagine his house as a history of Sicily–each century adding another piece in its own style with lots of accidental spaces caught inside like air bubbles in amber.

There are novels like that: old ones, perhaps *Don Quixote,* and at least one new one, Graham Swift's *Waterland.* And I can think of one wonderful story: Alice Munro's "Oranges and Apples", which starts in a mood or mode of chronicle of provincial life, but turns into something else and something else again: larva, chrysalis, imago. The last instar something so gorgeous you could never have guessed it from the first pages.

Would Aristotle or Poe have helped her? But that doesn't mean that they're not helpful to her or the rest of us on the many occasions of pondering what to do with the jumble of incidents and tones that we're trying to rewrite.

Perhaps these pieces of dogma are like saints for different perplexities: St. Antony of Padua for finding lost things, St. Blaise for curing sore throats, St. Christopher for traveling safely (though I hear he's been displaced, alas).

Everyone says "Tell the truth." But I have in mind Konstantin Stanislavsky.

I used to assign and still suggest Stanislavsky's *An Actor Prepares* to my writing classes. There are two main reasons. Stanislavsky gives a good argument against cliché. If you use a cliché in your preparation for a role, you put a roadblock in front of any further imagining. Clichés are vague, large, inert, and therefore terminal. The other reason is less a warning, more a positive aid. If a character in fiction is lifeless, it often helps to play the part. Do all the preparation Stanislavsky asks an actor to do. Imagine the character's life offstage. What does she eat?

How? What does she fear? How does she dress? How does she feel going home? etc., etc. Out of this imagining will come a hundred details, and usually one of them will provide a life-giving drop.

I had an odd experience with the narrator of a long story of mine called "Connaissance des Arts." He was an okay guy, but was neither hot nor cold. Perhaps I was afraid someone would think he was me. So I changed his clothes, put him in a good suit and a custom-made striped shirt with a white collar. I gave him narrow feet and put good shoes on them. I didn't need to mention any of this in the story. He began to act differently. The gulf that he perceived between him and his favorite student at the University of Iowa became more painful for him, at the same time his feelings for her became sharper. I don't know if the story is good, but it became more alive.

An Actor Prepares is a simply written series of lessons at a rhetorical level of *Dick and Jane*'s "See Spot run." It is a work of genius. But...I sometimes have misgivings about it. One is that Stanislavsky didn't have a great sense of humor. Chekhov kept writing him, when Stanislavsky was directing Chekhov's plays: "Please, Konstantin, it's meant to be funny." The other misgiving is that Stanislavsky seems to hold that the memory of one fear, for example, can animate the fear of the character to be portrayed. You might, relying only on your own emotions, inflate your jealousy at your junior high prom into Othello's. There is a danger of using emotions as isotopes or platonic ideals. It can work; I have only a misgiving about this, not an objection.

The antidote to this last misgiving about Stanislavsky's method, as valuable a tool as it often is, can be found in the work of another Russian, Vladimir Nabokov, specifically in *Speak, Memory*. Among the many, many things *Speak, Memory* is, it is a manual on the art of memory. Nabokov's memories are not interchangeable, although he could bestow them on certain of his characters as dangerous gifts. They are conjured for them selves, in all their infinite particularity. It is infinite particularity that is Nabokov's argument against cliché.

There is a wonderful chapter on his drawing teachers. Without deploying his whole pattern of development, from the facile and sweet to the labored and expressionistic to the precisely observed and rendered (so precise was Nabokov's observation and rendering that he was once employed by Harvard's Peabody Museum to do drawings of butterfly genitalia!), I'll simply characterize that chapter as perfect miniature commentary on the dialectic (how he would grind his teeth at that word) of becoming an artist, whether visual or verbal.

So there are at least two saints in this tell-the-truth-niche. Tell the truth, implore the intercession of one saint or the other or both, and tell it again. A tenor in an Italian town was called back for a third encore. "Thank you, thank you," he said, "But I can't–." A voice from the crowd called out, "You'll sing it again until you get it right!"

Tom Wolfe's dogma: "Be a reporter." Here's an easy one, but it comes up frequently enough to be worthwhile. Wolfe wrote an essay in *Harper's* magazine in 1989 on how to write a novel. In essence it said, "Go out and be a reporter. The material is out there! Get out of your ivory tower, stick a pencil stub behind your ear and do it the old-fashioned way. You could be Balzac, you could be Zola, you could be me!" There are some writers you'd like to see kicked in the pants in just this way.

I read a very good book (now out of print) several years ago: *Nimrod of the Sea* by William Morris Davis, a story of American whalemen. Every reportorial detail that is in *Moby Dick* is in there, and then some. In addition to harpooning, a Nantucket sleigh-ride, the tryworks etc, there are icebergs in the Bering Sea, surfing in Hawaii, and a wealth of other lore. But *Nimrod of the Sea* is no *Moby Dick.*

I like *Nimrod of the Sea.* It should be reprinted. But still, a first-rate way to learn the difference between very good reporting and the art of the novel is to read both books.

"Conventional narrative bores me." Robert Coover then went on to say, "You must experiment."

He was one of the smartest teachers at the University of Iowa when I was there. At that time it looked as if he, along with John Barth, would be the North American answer to Borges. It could still work out that way.

Both Coover and Barth appear in a dozen, no, a score of recent anthologies of short fiction. Their best stories are wonderful. The best of Barth is probably "Lost in the Fun House." It *is* experimental. It plays with language, with received ideas, with the convention of narrative, with the architecture of the fun house and the architecture of the very fiction we are reading. There is a host of Barth works on which the same descriptive label could be pinned. Some are good, some are sterile. All the smart stuff is there, but it's solving a chess problem.

I think the qualification of the command to experiment is this: variation for variation's sake, experiment for experiment's sake is for the notepad, for the sketchbook. Experiments work in art when they contain the same emotional charge that good fiction always has. Originality is not a sufficient condition for storytelling. When the experiment is attempted as a way to produce a charged state of being, so that less of the charge is lost in transmission, *then* you're trying for the big gold ring.

"Culture is local." William Carlos Williams was a pal of Ezra Pound. Ezra Pound whirled off to England and Italy, learned Latin, Italian, maybe Provençal, and delighted in Chinese poems. His allegiance, his literary allegiance, was European. In the *ABC of Reading,* a rich swath-cutting primer with a great reading list, Pound says intimidatingly that if you want to know poetry and don't know Latin and Provençal, you might still have some fun in English. He's not an antiquarian–he's in favor of writers who've brilliantly upset the applecart–but he harks back and abroad.

William Carlos Williams stayed home. He did do a young man's European tour, but then he set up in New Jersey and practiced medicine, wrote about Paterson, his patients, his home ground.

I like teaching Williams's *The Farmer's Daughters* because in those prose pieces he does find what is wonderful down the street, around the corner. There are famous stories in it—"The Use of Force," "The Girl with the Pimply Face"—but my favorite is "Old Doc Rivers," the life of an old-time country doctor, with a kind of genius and a terrible restlessness. (*The Farmer's Daughters* is also reassuring to students because some of the stories are great successes and some are instructive duds.)

Once again we have two patron saints. Do they cancel each other out? Is it an either/or?

I was wandering around Washington, D.C. one day, wondering why there's so little good fiction written about it. The good American political novels are set elsewhere. *All the King's Men* is set in Louisiana, other good political fiction comes from Boston, or Chicago. (There's a little bit of good stuff about journalism—a subculture that is local in the sense of sealed in and centripetal). It occurred to me that politicians, like most TV shows, are trying to write themselves as broadly appealing, and, because they aren't truthful, they end up as clichés. But then at my feet I saw another answer. In front of the National Theater there's a plaza on whose paving stones are inscribed quotations about Washington. The one on which I was standing said, "Washington—neither Rome or home."

I wish I'd said that. (When Oscar Wilde wistfully murmured that he wished he'd said a smart wisecrack he'd just heard, Whistler said to him, "You will, Oscar, you will.")

Washington, so far at least, hasn't been a matrix for either the Pounds or the William Carlos Williamses. (One footnote exception comes to mind, a good book of stories—*Lost in the City* by Edward P. Jones—which is set in Washington, but it is about black Washington, a population by and large excluded from the national media nonculture, but with a William Carlos Williams culture of its own.)

As to our two saints–Pound of Rome and Williams of home–there's another way of setting up the difference. It is the distinction between the tale and the modern short story. A tale occurs when someone leaves home, goes over the hills and far away, and comes back to tell the folks what amazing things are out there. A short story occurs when someone stays home and ponders local life until she can produce what is amazing about the things going on in her own culture, in her own words. Both the tale and the short story can be all the things our first eight points and counterpoints of dogma exhort us to write.

After considering these exhortations and their undertows, are we back where we started? Nobody thought that when you are facing the imperfect, half-alive matter you have committed to the page, that you could dial 1-800-OUR-DOGMA. As so often happens in law, the question isn't just what the laws are, but which ones apply to the case. Writing fiction–rewriting fiction–is trial and error, intuition and amended intuition. But in the effort to find your way through you own material, an application of one or another of these suggestions from our inherited lore may provide the right course correction.

Lincoln, Nebraska, 1992

JOHN CASEY is the author of *An American Romance, Testimony and Demeanor,* and *Spartina,* which won the National Book Award for fiction. A frequent contributor to such magazines as *The New Yorker, Sports Illustrated, Shenandoah,* and *Harper's,* Mr. Casey taught for twenty years at the University of Virginia. His new novel, set in Virginia, will be published this year, and the following year, the sequel to *Spartina.*

Interview

Marilynne Robinson

Tell us about us about your beginnings as a writer: What first made you want to write?

I was always interested in writing, I think. When I was a little kid, I read a great deal and wrote poetry. I don't know why this was my impulse, but it was. My brother was the same way about drawing and painting. He was my mentor, and he would give me books from the vantage of his greater maturity–Emily Dickinson's being one, the *Dialogues of Plato* being another, and so on. Those were the kinds of things that formed my ideas about what you would write if you were going to write. I realized at a certain point, I think when I was in high school, that my poetry was really very bad. I got around to fiction, finally, because I couldn't do what I wanted with poetry. What I'm typically trying to do is compensate myself for my inability to write poems. But there have been long periods in my life when I didn't write fiction or poetry, and I sometimes wonder, looking back, why during all that time I never doubted that I was actually a writer, although I was very secretive about it. I don't know why I always felt that was true.

There have been long periods between your books. One critic wrote that he felt your novel *Housekeeping* had been saved up over many years.

I think that I do have that habit of thinking things over. I watch things, in the way of somebody trying to make sense of them, and these things feed in to what I'm writing. When I was a child we lived in a very special sort of landscape. I was very aware of it, and watched it, because everyone in my family watched it. We lived in Idaho, just south of the Canadian border. It's very beautiful and mountainous, and for a long time it was very, very thinly settled. My great-grandparents were among the first white people to settle there, and we sort of collectively wondered why we were there.

That sounds like Fingerbone, the setting for *Housekeeping*.

Topographically, Fingerbone is very much like the town of Sandpoint where I grew up. There's a long bridge there, and as a little kid I was very aware always of trains coming and going. But the novel is fiction.

I started writing *Housekeeping* when I was in graduate school. While I was writing my dissertation–probably the longest thing I've ever written, on the historiographical traditions of Shakespeare's early history plays–people told me that writing that kind of scholarly work basically foreclosed the possibility of writing fiction. I didn't want that to be true so I would write extended metaphors from time to time, just to assure myself that I could still write in this other way. My undergraduate specialization had been in American literature and I was enormously interested in how those writers used figurative language as a sort of epistemological method.

I didn't think of the metaphorical passages I was writing as being particularly related to each other at all, but after I was done with my dissertation I took them out of the drawer and saw that they were very much related. So I put them together, and that was the point at which the figure of Sylvie came in. A lot of the things that are in *Housekeeping* are preoccupations that emerged from this kind of writing without any specific intentions—and they were preoccupations I wasn't particularly aware of, like housekeeping, and memory, and place.

What were your conscious concerns when you were writing the novel?
Housekeeping, among other things, is obsessed with nineteenth-century American literature. Since I thought I was writing an unpublishable book, I filled it with literary allusions to writers like Dickinson and Melville and Emerson and Thoreau. I had specifically in mind what I took to be the philosophical project of those writers. As I said, I thought they had done something incredibly interesting with figurative language that had not been carried on after them, and so I consciously took that up again.

Did you plot out your novel before sitting down to write it?
No. I don't plot things out. As Roethke said, I learn by going where I have to go, and I try to respond to what the fiction seems to be implying. So I didn't shape it in my mind, at least not consciously. I didn't know the ending of the novel, because one of the things that I did in the course of writing it was to try and evade my critical training; I didn't want to write it in the way a critic would write. I thought I was doing everything in the world to ensure that it would never be published, and that gave me enormous latitude: I didn't have to worry about what other people would think.

How do you create your fictional characters?
I'm in the middle of writing another novel and I'm noticing that one of the things that bothers me very much about fiction as it's normally practiced is that it seems as if the characterizations are terribly thin. The sense of what human beings are like is so reduced that it's almost not representational at all. My way of solving that problem in *Housekeeping* was to take what I considered to be dimensions of a single character and array them across a whole spectrum of characters. People, in their

behavior, make choices, so when we characterize them we do it in terms of how they act. But those same people have other impulses that they have decided to suppress, yet they are as much a part of their lives as the impulses they decide to act on. What you choose to do has a shadow of what you choose to forego.

In order to create that feeling of dimensionality, I simply split up one woman and made her into a group of women. The character I was primarily concerned about was Ruth. I wanted to make a narrator who would be completely compassionate, one who did not judge. I'm very fond of all my characters, and I don't make invidious comparisons between them, but Lucille is somebody who accepts the necessity of making judgments.

Did you set out to write about sisters?

I didn't intend to write about sisters. They're only related because that is a way of putting them in intimate connection with each other. The fact that they are versions of each other was established before the fact that in the fiction they are sisters. But I was always interested in watching sisters, perhaps because I didn't have one, and I was interested to find out how strong a notion that was for me. And here I am, working on a novel that has sisters in it also, which I hadn't intended to do.

Is writing about the family a subject of particular interest to you?

We talk about family all the time, to the point where if I hear the word "dysfunctional" once more I will die. One of the things that's strange to me about our society is that people act as if their families were held together from the outside. I think the essence of family is that you have to agree to it, and then supply, out of your imagination and capacity for loyalty, the contents of it. To a very large extent, it's an idea that is maintained by being cared for and elaborated upon *as an idea,* among the people who are involved in it. My family was very aware of itself as a family—very inclined to say that it had certain traits and features. When I was a kid growing up I was always being assured that I was taking after aunt so-and-so or had all the attributes of uncle so-and-so, and that sort of interested me. I think that these two motives are mutually present–mutually reinforcing–in the novel.

You write both fiction and nonfiction. Which do you enjoy the most? Is one genre more important to you than the other?
The pleasures don't loom large, frankly, in either case. I like to write them both, and I like to write them in association with each other. The culture of the nonfictional is a country in which writers actually think they're saying things that are true –a very naive idea. Then there's the country of fiction, and what's peculiar there is that writers imagine there's another place where people are saying things that are true. It's sort of like moving back and forth between dialects: the peculiarities of one sensitize you to the peculiarities of the other.

We've gotten into this corner where it's as if the purpose of art were to break down barriers or to shock, but that's not the primary object of anybody with serious aesthetic or philosophical engagement. I think that the first responsibility of a writer is the same as the first responsibility of any artist –which is to create something of interest and value, something that behaves in terms that are describable in the language of aesthetics. The responsibility of writers is to produce writing of quality, to think seriously about what they do and to simply produce the best quality of work they can.

Iowa City, Iowa, 1994

MARILYNNE ROBINSON is a professor at the Writers' Workshop at the University of Iowa. She is the author of the novel *Housekeeping*, and a book of nonfiction, *Mother Country: Britain, the Welfare State and Nuclear Pollution*, both of which were National Book Award finalists.

Entering Poetry

Philip Levine

Not until my thirteenth year did I fully discover the pleasures of solitude; this was at the same time I also began to discover the magic and variety of the natural world. That seems a little late in life, but I grew up in a city, one I liked, and my elders were seldom called upon to take me away for more than a day trip to a nearby lake or amusement park. At the age of eight my twin brother, Eddie, and I were sent to a dilapidated summer camp for several weeks. The food was so tasteless and meager we scarcely ate, and the evening we returned to town we greedily devoured my grandmother's heavy cooking only to spend a long night vomiting by turns in the bathroom. The next morning the family doctor was sent for, and my mother's fears were calmed when he informed her that such eruptions were general throughout Detroit as boys and girls returned from their various summer outings. Thereafter Eddie and I remained in town during the long summers.

As the years passed I began to find dinner increasingly difficult. It was the only time the family assembled, and thus it often became the arena for the resolution of daily grudges. I was as much at fault as anyone. I frequently ate in as slovenly and loud a manner as I could command, as though I intended to drive my mother and brothers away from the table. Only my fingernails were filthier than my language. It did no good to race through the meal. My mother was doing her best to bring us into harmony, and we were required to remain until the last morsel was consumed. Eddie was a very elegant eater; he no longer switched his knife and fork from hand to hand as I did. He ate slowly, methodically, and with great satisfaction, and he ate a lot. I envied his style and patience. Even after dinner, in the room we shared I found little peace. Although we were no longer addicted to torturing each other, as in years past, no true fellowship had replaced our rivalry. It should have, for we were both preoccupied for gaining revenge from all those who belittled or insulted us, from Adolf Hitler to our shop teacher. "I'll give no quarter and I'll take no quarter," Eddie stated with typical gusto. (He'd already discovered Sir Walter Scott.) I'd seen him fight and knew he was serious. When he got another boy down he would kick him with all his considerable might. Only the tallest and toughest of the Episcopal boys at our new school called him a dirty Jew.

The year was 1941. My mother had just purchased a house near the outskirts of the city located on an almost vacant block. There were similar square, two-storied houses on each side of ours and two houses directly across from ours and from the house of Steve Psaris, our neighbor to the north. There was also one house directly behind ours. To the east were two blocks of fields and then Livernois, a wide, four-lane avenue, famous for its profusion of used-car lots. To the west were two totally undeveloped blocks, still deeply wooded with maple, elm, and beech and thick underbrush. In my imagination this settlement of six families was a tiny America, an outpost of civilization between a vast open prairie and the mysterious darkness of a wilderness.

When I sneaked out of the house after dinner each night I headed directly for the security of the dense thickets and trees. Once into the woods I would make my way to one of my favorite trees, most often a large copper beech whose low branches spread out almost horizontally, and lean back and survey the night sky. There was no industry in this part of the city, and so the stars were visible and on some nights spectacular. One night I began to speak both to and of them. Immediately I felt something enormously satisfying about this speaking, perhaps because nothing came back in the form of an argument. It was utterly unlike any speaking I'd either heard or made before. I liked the way my voice, which was just changing, would gather itself around or within certain sounds, the "r" of "rains," the long open "o" sound of "moon." I would say "rain" and "moon" in the same sentence and hear them echo each other, and a shiver of delight would pass through me. On cloudy, starless nights, when the air seemed dense and close, I'd hurl my new voice out at the sky by saying, "The clouds obscure the stars," one tiny delicious sentence, but for the most part I was not brief. Best were those nights after a hard rain. In the darkness the smell of the wet earth would fill my head almost to the bursting point. "The damp earth is giving birth," I would say, and then in sentence after sentence I'd go on to list all that was being born within and outside me, though in the dense night I could hardly discern where I ended and the rest of the world began.

I was no longer addressing the stars, for often they had deserted me. Was I addressing God? I'm sure I was not, for I had no belief in a God who could hear me even though I was learning Hebrew and reading the Bible and discussing its deeper meanings each week with my instructor, a chubby-handed little man who was preparing himself for the rabbinate. Quite simply, Eddie and I had worked it out together and come to a complete accord: there was no God or any chosen people. "What the fuck were we chosen for?" Eddie would shout out after one of our frequent losing battles with the taller Episcopalians, most of whom were driven to school in long Lincolns or Packards, while we made the mile-and-a-half trek on foot even in the worst weather. No, I believe I was already a blooming Platonist addressing the complement, all that I was not and yearned to become. When I was in the crow's nest of my copper beech the wet-earth smells rose around me and the wind quivered the hard leaves and carried my voice out to the edges of the night; I could almost believe someone was listening and that each of my words, freighted with feeling, truly mattered. I was certain I was becoming a man.

One spring day, returning from school through the great prairie east of our house, I came across a wild iris, a tiny purple thing growing on its own, just a single bloom with no sign of a neighbor, doing its solitary best to enlighten the afternoon. I ran home and returned with a bucket and shovel from the garage. I dug up the iris, making sure to take plenty of dirt and being careful not to sever the roots. In our backyard I dug up a few square feet of sod near the back fence and planted the wildflower. I watered it carefully, but even by dinnertime it looked as though it had had it, so pitifully did it sag. By morning it was a goner. On Saturday I combed the open fields and found two more wild irises, I dug a second hole and planted the two side by side, this time preparing the ground with a dark, evil-smelling fertilizer I'd bought at Cunningham's Drug Store. I watered one flower hardly at all for fear I might have drowned the first iris. By later afternoon it was clear they'd both died. I asked the advice of Sophie Psaris, Steve's wife, who seemed able to make anything grow. She assured me that not even she could transplant a wildflower and make it grow. As a girl in Salonika, she'd fallen in love with the blood-red poppies that stained the meadows each April, but though she'd tried to get them to take hold in her mother's garden, she'd always failed. "Try rosebushes," she said. "The flowers are beautiful and they grow easily." I decided there was something proper about the irises' stubborn refusal to grow inside our fenced yard, something dignified in their preferring death to captivity. Never again would I interfere.

A week later, with money earned from washing windows, I bought my first rosebush, a little thorny stick of a thing with its dirt-encrusted roots wrapped in burlap. "You want something that will grow like mad?" said Bert, the little wizened Englishman who worked in the garden section of Cunningham's. For sixty-nine cents he let me have a mock orange. In no time at all, he assured me, it would be taller than I, but, then, I was still less than five feet tall. "Why do you call it a mock orange?" I asked. "Because that's its name. You see, it doesn't give any oranges; you can't grow oranges this far north. It's not even a tree–it's a shrub–but the blossoms look and smell like real orange blossoms."

The instructions for planting the rose spoke of "sandy loam" and the need to place the roots six to nine inches deep into this "sandy loam." After my disasters with the irises, I was hesitant and so took a handful of our backyard dirt to show Sophie. "Is this sandy loam?" I asked. She took a pinch from my open palm between her thumb and forefinger and smelled it and then put a few grains on her tongue and spit them out. "Pheelip," she said in her heavily accented English, "this is just dirt, you know, dirt that comes from the ground." This didn't really answer my question, so with no little trepidation I took a second handful to Cunningham's to show Bert. Was this in fact sandy loam? He stared at me in silence for half a minute and then cocked his head to one side. Why was I asking? I explained how the instructions had spoken of a six- to nine-inch hole in "sandy loam." "Where'd you get this?" he said. I told him I'd dug it out of a hole in my back yard. "Yes, of course you did," he said, "it's dirt, it'll do just fine. Call it 'sandy loam' if you'd like." He assured me that if I just planted the thing in a hole and gave it some water it would grow. "It's a lot less fussy than we are," he added.

Somewhat heartened, I returned home and planted the mock orange in the already fertilized hole that had failed the iris and planted the rose beside the fence separating our lot from Steve Psaris's driveway. I liked the way my hands smelled afterward. I washed away the grosser signs of their filthiness, but I was careful to leave just enough dirt under my fingernails so that whenever I wanted to I could catch a whiff of the earth's curious pungency that suggested both tobacco and rust. Though the soil of our backyard was a dull gray-brown, the perfume was a foxy red.

The rose especially was such a sad little thing that in spite of Bert's encouragement I was certain it would not survive, but within a week tiny reddish twigs began to jut out from the woody gray stick. I would press my thumb against the new thorns just to feel their sharpness against my skin. Eddie liked to speak of something he called a "blood oath," a vow taken by two strong men and sealed by the mixing of their blood. At the time he was reading Dumas and Sabatini and often spoke also of taking fencing lessons, though we knew no one in Detroit who gave them. One day I considered puncturing my skin against the largest of the thorns, but I stopped short of this gesture. Sophie had assured me the buds would come as they had on their bushes. I knew from watching them they would transform themselves from hard green almond-shaped stones to the swelling red-tipped about-to-be-flowers.

One late May morning, I glanced out of the back window of the breakfast nook to discover the mock orange in bloom. Caught up in the excitement of the beginning of the baseball season, I'd not been paying attention and was taken by surprise. There were suddenly more than a dozen tiny blossoms and a rich, deep perfume that reminded me of the perfume of my Aunt Belle, my mother's youngest sister. After school I cut a small branch of three blossoms and placed it in a glass of water and set it in the middle of the dining-room table. To my surprise, that evening no one noticed it, and dinner passed with Eli, my older brother, discussing his plans for a camping trip in northern Canada. I listened in silence, and when the others had left the table I dropped the little branch down the front of my shirt.

The days were lengthening, and it was still light out when I sneaked out of the house after helping with the dishes. I made my way to the deepest center of the woods and climbed a young maple tree and gazed up into the deepening sky above. I must have dozed off for a few minutes because quite suddenly the stars emerged in a blacker sky. Although I did not know their names—in fact, I did not even know they had names—I began to address them quietly, for I never spoke with "full-throated ease" until hidden by the cover of total darkness. A soft wind shook the leaves around me. From my own hands I caught the smell of earth and iron, which now I carried with me at all times. I reached down my shirt and extracted the mock-orange branch and breathed in the deep feminine odors while between thumb and forefinger I fretted the blossoms until they fell apart. I began then to address my own hands, which seemed somehow to have been magically transformed into earth. For the first time a part of me became my night words, for now the darkness was complete. "These hands have entered the ground from which they sprang," I said, and, tasting the words, I immediately liked them and repeated them, and then more words came that also seemed familiar and right. Then I looked on the work my hands had wrought, then I said in my heart, As it happened to the gardener, so it happened to me, for we all go into one place; we are all earth and return to earth. The dark was everywhere, and as my voice went out I was sure it reached the edges of creation. I was sure too my words must have smelled of sandy loam and orange blossoms. That was the first night of my life I entered poetry.

In the spring of 1952 in Detroit, I was working at Chevrolet Gear and Axle, the "abandoned factory" of a poem in my first book, *On the Edge,* and I hated the job more than any I'd had before or have had since, not only because it was so hard, the work so heavy and monotonous that after an hour or two I was sure each night that I would never last the shift, but also because it was dangerous. There in the forge room, where I worked until I was somehow promoted to a less demanding, equally boring job, the stock we handled so gingerly with tongs was still red-hot as we pulled it from the gigantic presses and hung it above us on conveyors that carried our handiwork out of sight. Others had mastered the art of handling the tongs loosely, the way a good tennis player handles his racquet as he approaches the net for a drop volley, applying just enough pressure not to let go and not enough to choke it. Out of fear I squeezed for all I was worth, and all the good advice, the coaching I received from my fellow workers, was of no use.

One night just after we'd returned to our machines after the twenty-minute break, the guy I was working with–a squat broad-shouldered young black man whose energy and good spirits I'd admired for weeks–tapped me on the shoulder and indicated with a gesture that I should step aside. Together we'd been manning a small punch press; he handed me the stock that came along a conveyor, I inserted it in the machine, had it punched, and then hung it on another conveyor. On this occasion he said nothing, though even if he had I wouldn't have heard him over "the oceanic roar of work." He withdrew a short-handled sledgehammer from inside his shirt and, gripping it with both hands, hammered furiously at the press's die. He then inserted a piece of stock in the machine, tripped the button that brought the press down, and leaped aside before the press could whip the metal out of his hands. The press froze. I went to summon the foreman, Lonnie, while my partner disposed of the hammer. Lonnie took one look at the machine and summoned two men senior to him, or so I assumed since they arrived dressed in business suits. For twenty minutes they searched the area. I finally figured out that they were looking for the instrument with which the press had been sabotaged. Then they separated us and grilled me. There was no question, they assured me, that the press bore the marks of violence. What had "the nigger" done? I answered that I'd seen nothing out of the ordinary, the machine just broke down, almost tore my hands apart. Oh they looked at each other, I wanted it that way. Well, they could certainly accommodate me. Before the night was over, I was back on the "Big Press," handling those red-hot sections of steel, my hands stiffening and kinking inside the huge gauntlets. Within a few days I was once again dreaming of fire as my hands gnarled even in sleep. I lasted a few more weeks, and when it became obvious that the "Big Press" was mine forever, I quit.

Five years later, while living in Palo Alto, California, on a writing grant from Stanford University, I received an article clipped from a Detroit newspaper and mailed to me. It told of the closing of Chevrolet Gear and Axle; its functions had been moved to a new, highly automated plant near Pontiac. I had already tried at least a dozen times to capture the insane, nightmarish quality of my life at Chevy: that epic clanging of steel on steel, the smell of the dead rats we poisoned who crawled off into their secret places and gained a measure of revenge, the freezing winds at our backs as winter moved through the broken windows, the awesome heat in our faces, those dreamlike moments when the lights failed and we stood in darkness and the momentary silence of the stilled machines. In the springlike winter of 1957, sitting in the little poetry room of the Stanford library, which was mine alone each morning, half a country and a universe away from Chevy, I could recall almost without hatred that old sense of utter weariness that descended each night from my neck to my shoulders, and then down my arms to my wrists and hands, and how as the weeks had passed my body had changed, thickening as though the muscles and tendons had permanently swelled, so that I carried what I did with me at all times, even when I lifted a pencil to write my poems. It was not the thickening heaviness of myself I tried to capture in my abandoned-factory poem—I only managed a glimmer of that—for I was determined to say something about the importance of the awfulness I had shared in and observed around me, a worthy aim, certainly, but one that stopped me from writing the poetry of what I had most deeply and personally experienced.

Seven years later, in the spring of 1964, I was living in a large airy house in Fresno, California, a house of beautiful slow dawns. Each morning I would waken early, before six, and watch the light—yellow and pale green as it filtered through the leaves of the sycamore outside my bedroom—transform the darkness into fact, clear and precise, from the tiled floor to the high, sloping, unfinished wooden ceiling. It was a real California house. I would rise, toss on a bathrobe, and work at my poems for hours seated at the kitchen table, work until the kids rising for school broke my concentration. To be accurate, I would work unless the morning were spoiled by some uncontrollable event, like a squadron of jet fighters slamming suddenly over the low roofs of the neighborhood, for we lived less than a quarter mile from a National Guard airfield.

One morning in April of that year I awakened distressed by a dream, one that I cannot call a nightmare, for nothing violent or terribly unpleasant had occurred in it. I dreamed that I'd received a phone call from a man I'd known in Detroit, Eugene Watkins, a black man with whom I'd worked for some years in a grease shop there. Eugene was a tall, slender man, ten years older than I, and although he had his difficulties at home he rarely spoke of them. In fact he rarely spoke. What I remember most clearly about working beside him was that I never like schlepping or loading or unloading in tandem with him because he had a finger missing on his left hand, and I had some deep-seated fear that whatever had caused that loss could easily recur, and I didn't want the recurrence to take some treasured part of myself. The dream was largely a phone conversation, one in which I could see Eugene calling from a phone booth beside U.S. 99 in Bakersfield, 120 miles south of where I lived. He'd called to tell me he was in California with his wife and daughter. They'd driven all the way from Detroit and had just arrived. They wanted to know what they should do and see while they were in the West. As I babbled on about the charms of Santa Monica, L.A.'s Miracle Mile, the fashionable restaurants neither they nor I could afford, the scenic drive up U.S. 1 to Big Sur, I knew that what Eugene was actually seeking was an invitation to visit me. I even mentioned the glories of Yosemite and Kings Canyon National Park–neither more than an hour from where

I lived–and yet I never invited him. Finally he thanked me for all the information I'd given him, said good-bye, and quietly hung up. In the dream I saw him leave the phone booth and shamble, head down, back to the car, exactly as I would have in his place. I awakened furious with myself for my coldness, my lack of generosity, my snobbery. Why, I asked myself, had I behaved this way? Was it because Eugene was black? Several black friends had visited my house. Because he was working-class? I was living in a largely working-class neighborhood. (Who else has an airfield at the end of the block?) Did I think I was so hot with my assistant professorship at a second-rate California college, with my terrific salary that was probably no more than Eugene earned? Was I trying to jettison my past and join the rising tide of intellectuals, car salesmen, TV repairmen, and bank managers who would make it to the top? What the hell was I becoming?

It finally occurred to me that I had not rejected Eugene, my past, the city of my birth, or anything. I had had a dream, and that dream was a warning of what might happen to me if I rejected what I'd been and who I was. The kids were up and preparing for school, so I climbed back in bed with my yellow legal pad and my pen. I was in that magical state in which nothing could hurt me or sidetrack me; I had achieved that extraordinary level of concentration we call inspiration. When I closed my eyes and looked back into the past, I did not see the blazing color of the forges of nightmare or the torn faces of the workers. I didn't hear the deafening ring of metal on metal, or catch under everything the sweet stink of decay. Not on that morning. Instead I was myself in the company of men and women of enormous sensitivity, delicacy, consideration. I saw us touching each other emotionally and physically, hands upon shoulders, across backs, faces pressed to faces. We spoke to each other out of the deepest centers of our need, and we listened. In those terrible places designed to rob us of our bodies and our spirits, we sustained each other.

The first lines I wrote were for Eugene Watkins. I imagined us together in the magical, rarefied world of poetry, the world I knew we would never enter. Although it's snowing there, when we leave the car to enter the unearthly grove, no snow falls on our hair or on the tops of our shoes because "It's the life of poems;/the boughs expansive, our feet dry." But of course that was not the world I was returning to; I wanted to capture in my poetry the life Eugene and I had shared, so before the poem ("In a Grove Again") ends, the grove transforms itself into any roadside stop where two guys might pause to take a piss.

Meanwhile back in the car there are talismans:

> A heater, the splashed entrails of newspapers,
> A speedometer that glows and always reads 0.
> We have not come here to die. We are workers
> And have stopped to relieve ourselves, so we sigh.

I remained in bed much of that week. The poems were coming, and for reasons I couldn't explain, I felt my inspiration had something to do with the particular feel and odor of the bed. While there I wrote most of the Detroit poems that appear in my second book, *Not This Pig.* I believe that they were the first truly good poems I'd written about the city. They are by no means all sweetness and light. There was and still is much that I hate about Detroit, much that deserves to be hated, but I had somehow found a "balanced" way of writing about what I'd experienced; I'd tempered the violence I felt toward those who'd maimed and cheated me with a tenderness toward those who had touched and blessed me.

Sacramento, California, 1992

PHILIP LEVINE is the author of several books of poetry, including *Ashes* and *What Work Is* which both won National Book Awards. He studied with John Berryman and Yvor Winters and until recently taught at the university in Fresno, California. The preceding essay was included in Mr. Levine's most recent book of prose, *The Bread of Time: Toward an Autobiography.*

A reading at Rizzoli Bookstore

The Book Tour

E. Annie Proulx

There is a figure of the writer in the public imagination—a black-clad eccentric who writes with an auk plume and only comes into the light of day to bank heavy royalty checks which are wasted on drinks and trips to Tierra del Fuego.

There is a good deal of truth to this. But how many recognize that there is another, darker side to the writing life—risk, stress, and peril? You may have noticed how often a new book, usually a first novel or a collection of short stories or poems, appears, followed by three or four decent notices saying, "Thumbs up! Virgil Blitz is a writer to watch!" yet a few months later the book is gone, off the shelves, no paperback appears and the name Virgil Blitz is never seen nor heard again. I can tell you something—Blitz is dead in a ditch somewhere, adrift on an ice floe, trampled in a Missouri hog panic. Another writer lost. These disappearances—I believe there actually is a writer named Virgil Blitz who has a book entitled *Our Disappearing Authors* coming out after it runs in *The New Yorker* in thirty-one installments—these disappearances occur most often during the research stage of a book or in the peculiar weeks following its publication, when the author goes a-roving on that thing known as "the book tour." These are the dangerous times, and they are part of what is so blithely referred to as "the writing life."

When I first started going to Newfoundland to work on *The Shipping News,* I went with a friend. (He thought we were on a fishing trip.) It was an unsatisfactory experience, partly because of two weeks of gale-force winds and heavy rain which failed to repel the swarms of blackflies and mosquitoes, but also because, according to my friend–I am a sound sleeper–bears romped through our first campsite while my friend shouted "Wake up! Wake up!" My silence made him believe the bears had already done their foul work and, unsatisfied, were coming for him. At another camp a moose walked on the end of my friend's tent–the head end. His last straw was drawn when we anchored just offshore fishing for arctic char and a rubber dinghy pulled up alongside. In it was an advanced lunatic who described himself as a furnace salesman, then began to rave about the evil in the world. We tried to get away, but he followed, and after an hour of watery flight and pursuit, we hauled our boat up onto the shore. He hauled his up as well, exhorting us to give up our sinful ways and buy a furnace. Over dinner that evening my friend said he had to go home–1,500 miles away–because he thought he had left the bathtub faucet running.

A few months later I went back to Newfoundland alone, planning to stay at bed-and-breakfast outfits along the way. The first was run by an older couple, the woman rather stout and blustery, her husband blind from a woods accident years before. The guest room was tiny, about 6 x 8, barely large enough for the single cot and the twelve blankets on it. The walls were painted Dynamo Magenta. There was a ceiling bulb worked by a string, and a hook on the back of the door for one's clothes. Those were the amenities. Breakfast the next morning was a cup of tea, one bag spliced between three cups, and tiny bowl of gray porridge. As I sat sipping my tea, trying to make it last, for I doubted more would be coming my way, the husband, his right hand loosely clenched, made his way to the table and sank into his chair. He growled something that sounded like "smudgepots 'bout done," and his wife turned up the radio to a roar. I glanced up and was treated to the sight of the husband placing his glass eye on the table next to his teacup. Whether he took it out at night along with his false teeth, or whether it fell out in bed by itself and had been rolling around between them through the night I do not know. I rose, paid my bill and departed before he could dip it in his tea and pop it back in the socket.

My next stop was more exciting. The weather had gone cold and rainy again as it does in Newfoundland, and I pulled in at this second B&B anticipating a hot bath and a hot toddy. Before I could get my bag out of the truck a woman came flying down the steps and said, "Let me show you the furnace!" I am not one to resist local folkways, so I followed her into a cellar with a low ceiling where there was an immense oil furnace that went back into the bedrock. It bristled with all manner of switches and flanges, gauges and red buttons labeled DANGER. Somehow I knew from whom she had purchased it.

"You got to 'old down the backpressure feed switch behind THAT, whilst you gives this un a jab, after you gets the pilot on again as the wind blows it out pretty good. Come on up now, I'll show you the rest." I followed her upstairs and got a very full tour–where the linens were kept, where the pancake griddle was, both the bathrooms and why one toilet would not flush, the clothesline, the old washing machine, the broken binoculars, the silver jelly spoons, and was told that two miles up the road a woman keeps goats and that's where I should go for more milk when I ran out, and be sure to pasteurize it, and it was $40 for a double and the phone might ring with more reservations, and here were the keys, she was off to Labrador and would be back in two weeks, nothing to worry about but the furnace if the wind blew out the pilot light. As it happened, the furnace did go out, not because the wind extinguished the pilot light, but because it ran out of oil. I got little writing done, but

I learned something both of the Newfoundland character and oil furnaces.

The book tour takes one around unexpected corners, especially when dates and accommodations have to be changed on the road. Around the time my first novel, *Postcards,* came out, I had to go to Wyoming and my publisher arranged a sort of mix-it-and-match-it tour. I drove my battered old pickup. One of the stops was St. Paul, Minnesota, and because I was running a day late, delayed by something in Iowa, the hotel reservations were changed. I had the name of the new place I was to stay and directions to get there scribbled on the back of an envelope, and that's all I knew. The Drover's Inn. About an hour out of St. Paul it started to rain–it always rains on book tours–a particularly greasy rain that smeared the windshield and coated the road with a substance like diluted lard. I reached the turn-off for St. Paul, but the instructions were to keep driving. On and on I went, past St. Paul and in an ominous southeastern direction. On this side of the Rockies the worst part of most cities is to the southeast because of the prevailing drainage. About fifteen miles later, following the scribble on the back of the envelope, I found myself in a pungent district of low-slung bars, railroad yards, pens, chutes, and mean streets. There it was, the Drover's Inn, right handy to the stockyards for the cattle shippers who made up the regular clientele and those attentive to all their needs. And I stayed there even though I do not own a pair of fishnet stockings. There was not an empty room in Minneapolis nor St. Paul except for the Drover's Inn because of a wrestling convention. The same old story, sport before art.

A few weeks later I read at a bookstore in Wyoming. There were not many people at the reading–maybe twenty–but all of them seemed terrifically excited and sat on the edges of their chairs twitching and writhing and sneaking looks at papers in their hands. They leaned forward eagerly, yet I got the impression they weren't hearing a word. After about fifteen minutes I was discouraged and stopped reading, made my way back toward the Chardonnay and cheddar—but sat down when people went "Shh!" A young woman who had been sitting in the front row got up and read a poem about her first airplane ride, a poem that went on for frozen centuries of time. She barely finished when another one jumped up and launched into a searing prose description of sex with a teenage cowboy. And so it went, until the entire audience, made up of local writers, had read their stuff.

Travel, any kind of travel, is unnerving experience. Drive and there are the serial killer highways, the chance of running out of gas at midnight in Idaho, sticking in mud wallows, dodging tornadoes or outrunning blizzards, eating cruel food in Mud Butte or Biloxi. Fly, and it is paralysis in boa-constrictor seats, headache from oxygen deprivation, the salmonella sandwich, babble of seatmate who has just started a religious cult and needs followers, ice on the wings, lost luggage. Last spring I got the flu simultaneously with a strep throat, a sinus problem and a double ear infection. I was only half recovered when the book tour began. My ears crackled and echoed. Flying was impossible. It had to be the train. Amtrak.

The trip west was dismal but not perilous. There is nothing like traveling by train; all the socio-industrial crap of North America is visible as in no other form of travel: shacks, trash, tenements, discarded machinery, bus graveyards, ganglia of transmission towers, those pointed gravel storage sheds like enormous brassiere cups, generating stations that turn fog purple, drunk people in the weeds, iridescent wetlands that serve as combination swamp-and-appliance-disposal depots. Yet the trouble came on the return, the so-called Lake Shore Express—the name is a far-fetched conceit—heading east out of Chicago.

I fell asleep a few hours after the train pulled out and enjoyed an unusually restful night. I woke the next morning thinking that Amtrak must have discovered the secret of perfect sleeping-car suspension, and didn't quite take it in when the car attendant said we were still in Toledo, had been in Toledo since eleven o'clock the night before. There's a joke about a Texan trying to impress a New Englander with the size of his state. "Y' know," he says, "you kin boa'd the train in Dallis and twena-foah houas lateh you still in Tixas." It was like that. You board the train in Toledo and ten hours later you're still in Toledo. The car attendant handed me a paper cup of cool coffee and said that a tug was stuck under the railroad bridge over the Maumee River and nothing could get it unstuck, nothing, and that they were waiting for a brace of powerful tugs to come down from Detroit and tear it loose. Hours passed. No one knew anything. An old railroad tradition. Because there was no cellular phone on this train scores of furious passengers got off and went into the station, where they stood in line to use the only pay phone in working order to explain to the boss or spouse that although they should have been in Boston by now they were still–ha ha–in Toledo, home of the Detroit Tiger's minor league team, the Toledo Mud Hens. The ticket seller in the station shrugged and said the same thing had happened in November. More passengers got off to make more phone calls. Suddenly, with a lurch, the train went forward. The bridge was open. Once started the train did not stop, not even for the shouting passengers running down the platform. On the train itself the club car attendant was giving away packets of stale peanuts, Amtrak's solace to enraged passengers.

But now the train had lost its slot in the great flow of rail traffic, and nothing was going to work for it. In Rochester there was a four-hour delay; of the two eastbound tracks ahead, one was flooded and on the other a freight train had derailed and behind it seven other freights had right of precedence over us. Again and again the train stopped and waited, no one knew what for. Darkness fell once more. I had a terrific headache. And the train ran out of food.

Late this second night the train halted yet again in some nameless station in upstate New York and stood panting while nothing happened. After an hour and a half, a dozen taxis pulled up. We hungry passengers saw the train chief counting out money to the leader of the taxis. Then men brought dozens of large boxes to the train–the unmistakable salty, greasy aroma of Kentucky Fried Chicken filled the air as the taxis drove away. Yet the train *did not move,* and in another hour more taxis came, this time bearing a new train crew and union officials. There was more shouting. From this point on the train crew switched at every stop, although the sleeping-car attendants, reeling with fatigue after two sleepless nights, were not relieved. And at every stop passengers jumped off and ran for the airport.

The sleeping-car attendant was strung-out and crazy. He seemed at the end of his rope. From behind my green curtain I overheard a second attendant speak to him in the corridor.

"It can't last forever."

"It already has," said the first, then added, "I'm going to change my clothes." I heard him go into the empty roomette across the corridor.

After a few minutes I took an aspirin bottle from my purse and opened it. The lid cracked up noisily and the aspirins rattled. From the corridor the second attendant shouted. "John! What are you taking?"

"What?"

"What are you taking? I heard the pills rattle, goddammit. You better not be taking anything!"

"What are you talking about?" Their voices had a delirious, feverish quality.

"John! Open up. Hey, open up." The door slid open and the second attendant went inside. Their conspiratorial voices were clearly audible.

"I'll tell you something, John." His voice dropped. "Twelve hours overtime, that's like two days' pay! Two days' pay! God, I hope something else happens. Hey, Johnny, did you call up Carmen?"

But you're not interested in the rest of that conversation.

Gradually a terrible knowledge came. Somehow, in Chicago, I had boarded the Train from Hell on its endless, circling route, clanking and lurching through dirty days and nights until the universe ran down, and then on into the void.

Another morning came. All hope of making connections lost to those still on the train. The sleeping-car attendants were zombies. Passengers were choosing strange new destinations that had nothing to do with their former lives. A kind of euphoria had set in. "Let me off in New York, haven't been there in years." "I was going to Schenectady, but I'll think I'll take Boston now." I had been headed to Montreal, but decided to switch to Springfield, Massachusetts with connections to White River Junction, roughly thirty miles from where I lived. Amtrak claimed a taxi would be in Springfield to take the northbound refugees to White River, and a vehicle was actually there. We staggered from the train and six of us packed ourselves into a rump-sprung private car driven by a 300-lb. woman. I sat between a homeopathic physician who entertained us with accounts of astounding herbal cures and a pair of teen sweethearts who kissed and fondled. The radio played Rush Limbaugh all the way. It was an eternity until I was in the Polka Dot diner eating burned eggs and waiting for a friend to pick me up.

Some of my book-travel nightmares are my own fault. Once I forgot to set my watch back an hour and ended up in downtown Chicago at five o'clock on Friday evening of Memorial Day weekend in a freak hailstorm on a route undergoing heavy reconstruction. I experienced a compelling urge–I think it's called freeway syndrome–to get out and run toward the horizon across the hoods of the million stalled cars. And a few years ago, ready to board a flight to Dublin to receive a literary prize, it was only as I stepped up to the Aer Lingus check-in counter that I remembered I had forgotten to renew my passport.

The poison ivy of the Ozarks, thin oxygen at high altitude, a plate of suspicious emu sausage in Sydney, a ride in a float plane over the wilderness of Maine with a pilot who kept dozing off, three hundred miles of black-ice road in January in Newfoundland, rattlesnakes on a Wyoming stream bank–all were part of my recent writing life. Sometime, if I don't make it back, please tell my story to Virgil Blitz.

New York, New York, 1994

E. ANNIE PROULX is the author of a collection of short stories, *Heart Song*; and two novels, *Postcards* and *The Shipping News*. The latter received the National Book Award for fiction and the Pulitzer Prize. Her new novel, *Accordion Crimes,* will be published this year.

Interview

Louis Begley

Have books always played an important part in your life?
There is no time I can remember when I wasn't interested in reading. When I was a little child, I was read to, things that were very good–there was a good children's literature in Poland, and my mother read very well. I learned how to read fluently myself by the time I was five or six. My childhood was not exactly a normal childhood because of the war in Europe, and I went to school very little: I went for one year to what might be described as the first grade, and then I did not go to school again until the first year of the *gimnazjum,* which is comparable to high school. So there was a long period when reading was my principal occupation and my central pleasure. Writing little stories and poems came as part of learning. I was tutored during the war–both a teacher and my mother taught me–and I would be asked to write various things, and in this way I became accustomed to composition.

When I finally began to go to school continuously, after I arrived in the United States, it turned out that, while I was a good student in all subjects, paradoxically I did best in English. I was encouraged to write stories, which I did. Then I went to Harvard College and took writing courses until I had a revelation that

I had absolutely nothing to write about. I did not write poetry again, and did not write any fiction until 1989.

What made you decide to become a lawyer?

Like many young people who suddenly find that they have to earn their living, I had to ask myself, How are you going to do it? I was then in the United States Army and it was perfectly clear to me that I did not want to become a professional soldier. And I did not want to become a physician, which was what my father was, because I'm not much drawn to being with sick people. I had very little imagination about jobs, I thought I had no commercial instincts, and I had not yet become a good cook, so it came to me that a perfectly plausible profession was being a lawyer. It was all the more plausible since I knew nothing about what lawyers do.

A fortuitous decision!

It turned out to be. I have enjoyed my profession enormously and continue to enjoy it, and I think I'm good at it. I like legal writing, and making sure it's put together in a way that is both effective in conveying what one wants to say and aesthetically pleasing.

So, you have always been a writer?

I've not been a writer of fiction all my life. As I said, I wrote fiction and some poetry when I was a boy and an adolescent, but I stopped at the end of my junior year in college. But I was a writer during those years lost to fiction, because lawyers of my sort in fact spend a great deal of every day writing. Only, one writes other things: letters of advice, memoranda, law briefs, contracts, documents designed to bind people to each other or to convince people of this or that. So I've never not been writing.

How did you then return to fiction and write your first novel, *Wartime Lies*?

I had written what became the introduction and also a part of the first chapter, but at the time I imagined that it would be much more a book about my father than a book about the Second World War. And then I went on a sabbatical leave in 1989 and dusted off those pages, and I thought they were all right. But, as I read them, it became obvious to me that they were leading in a different direction: I had to ask myself how one would have become a man, after having been a boy of the sort I had been. The question of what had happened to the father of that boy, how his life had been bent by the war years, was one I decided I would deal with at some later time, if ever. This was not completely logical; it was a choice I cannot very well explain; I just had a strong feeling that I had found the direction I wanted to go in.

Then I thought about the shape of the book, because I don't believe in automatic writing. I can't write without know ing what is going to be on the next page. I rewrote the pages I already had and continued every day, keeping the shape of the book in mind, until the first draft of the novel was written.

Why did you choose to have two narrators in the novel?
That's the whole point of the book. It's a meditation by a man who has survived the war and has arrived at a form of accommodation with his present life, and at the same time has never made peace with the past and what his childhood had been. It is a reasonable choice, though, to tell about the childhood with the voice of the young boy; I thought it was the purest way of telling his story. But it would have been meaningless without the framework of a grown man, or perhaps the author, looking back on the boy.

Tell us about the boy, Maciek.
Maciek is Maciek because of the old song. I was haunted by the willingness of that little Maciek to sing and dance his heart out as long as the music plays. It seemed to me a good metaphor for the boy in my book. He was neither particularly good, nor particularly simple, nor a particularly easy child. Sexuality is

a very strong component of childhood, and I wondered what would be the effect of living in close quarters with someone like [his aunt] Tania. I wondered what degree of introspection and self-examination would, in these circumstances, be part of the childhood of a boy who was not, even at the beginning, a very simple child.

How do you see Tania?
Tania is an idealization of things observed. She is a heroine, and she is made of my dreams, as is the grandfather.

The grandfather's death was one of the most horrifying moments in the novel.
For me, too. I wept when I wrote those pages.

Was writing about a family important to you in *Wartime Lies*?
I was very much interested in the relationship between the little boy and his aunt—the mutual dependence, how a little boy is attracted by a woman's powerful physical magnetism, how he becomes a partner in the struggle to survive. I was interested in dominance, and resistance to dominance, and how a child's character is bent in a certain direction because of the influence of an adult. Then, in the case of the grandfather, I was interested in the phenomenon of the pure love of a child for an older person, a love which is without constraints—the movement of the heart toward someone who is admirable and good. The grandfather is a splendid fellow. The fact that I was a recent grandfather myself—my grandson was born two years before I began to write *Wartime Lies,* and my granddaughter was born in July of 1989, the year the novel was written—had a little something to do with my interest in the relationship between a child and his grandfather.

The novel's narrator says that he avoids books about the Holocaust. Do you think there is a Holocaust literature?
I really don't know. I don't consider myself to be part of that. I think that the classification of books is very much a matter of

what label booksellers put on a bookshelf–gardening books, self-help books, whatever. I am very skeptical about categories. I think that my book is about a little boy and some people around him who lived in Poland from 1933 to 1945. That's what it is about. It is not a Holocaust book.

Why did you chose the title *Wartime Lies*?
Actually, I intended to call the book *The Education of a Monster,* but my family wouldn't let me. They said it wasn't a title that would sell.

In fact, what is important in your title is "Lies," not "Wartime."
That's precisely right.

Do you feel an author has obligations to his readers?
I have an obligation to myself, which is to write as well as I can, and never to depart from the truth. And the truth is not an autobiographical truth, which interviewers are usually after, but an emotional truth. My obligation is not to tell things that aren't right from my perspective and experience–not to tell things that I've simply invented in order to fill pages. I've never done it and I never will. What I write comes out of some crucible inside me. And I never, never want to write a bad sentence, if I can help it.

New York, New York, 1994

LOUIS BEGLEY is a partner of Debevoise & Plimpton, specializing in international law. He is the author of the novels *Wartime Lies,* which was nominated for a National Book Award, *The Man Who Was Late,* and *As Max Saw It.*

Breathing Space

Bob Shacochis

A while back I was standing behind a lectern at a bookstore in Manhattan, reading from my first novel, *Swimming in the Volcano,* which had just been published. A CBS-TV crew was there, taping my performance–if you want to call it that–yet I had an uneasy feeling, accurate, as it turned out, that the segment would never air; my material was not the sort that complements lazy Sunday-morning yawns and breakfast in bed: neither sexy nor charming, neither warm nor light, and certainly not domestic.

Just as you have to teach yourself to write a novel, you also have to learn, in this age of entertainment and self-promotion, how to read from it in an effective, representative, though digestible and engaging manner. I had chosen an intensely introspective passage to read, an excerpt in which the character Issac Knowles–a young West Indian unjustly imprisoned by the authorities–sits in a damp, dimly lit dungeon cell, meditating on his fate and ultimately, counting his blessings. Issac's counting evolves into a transitional device, carrying him away from the interior world of precious memories into an exterior world without mercy, where he will soon be brutally beaten and, the reader can presume, killed. I had chosen that particular chapter to read with the hope that it answered the question implied by the midtown Manhattan venue: *Writer, who are you?* and I would respond, through my reading, *This is me*: Here is the work that best exemplifies my skills as a writer; my esthetic value system, which has its source in the texture and layering of language and imagery and the complexity of human experience. Here is the work that evokes my moral and political universe; the work that most clearly resonates with the life of my imagination. *This is me,* I hoped to say to my audience. *This is the best I can do.*

My wife, my editor, and my agent happened to be standing off to the side, behind a rack of books, listening. It was the first time any of them had heard me read from the novel and, at some point during the event, my wife told me later, she turned to my editor and whispered, half-jokingly but also of course half-seriously, "I think Bob might be an idiot savant."

As far as I know, my editor did not disagree, but either way, she understood what my wife was saying. The person who knew me best, who had spent seventeen years by my side, who continuously scrutinized me in a spouse's effort to determine the precise nature of whom it was she lived with and loved–this woman knew that in my everyday life, as practiced by my quotidian self, there was scant evidence to suggest that I was indeed the person who had written what I was reading from the lectern. Even in the eyes of my most loyal and intimate witness, whatever was at the core of my life as a writer remained obscure.

"I don't know where it comes from," she said as we left the bookshop that evening. I nodded, flattered and grateful and yet perplexed.

The fact is, I don't know either–unless what we're really talking about is the prosaic mystery of work, hard effort, the type of work anybody does, in any walk of life, when they care deeply about the value and the meaning of their vocation.

That's the short answer–I know it's not especially revealing. On the other hand, I sense, though I've never bothered to articulate it before, either to myself or others, that behind this simple query, *Where does it come from?* there exists a shadowy but real and definite world, with its own singular history and traditions and rules, its failures and successes. The truth is, I do know where it comes from, but in a vague way. And I've always felt that the access I have to that place, and to the person or personality who resides there, is astonishingly limited. The psychic distance I travel between one place and the other–between my life upstairs, where I cook and eat and sleep and watch television and live with my wife, and my life downstairs, where I sit at my desk late at night and write–often makes me feel like an actor. Which life is which–that's what I don't know. The duality is like a willed yet benevolent form of schizophrenia. Sometimes, it unnerves me.

Sometimes I feel an urgent, panicky need to be protected from it, that hazardous nighttime sea that for me is creativity and the writing life. I'm not at all convinced that I can face its challenges, face its secrets, and survive. And yet risking survival–physical, professional, intellectual, emotional, spiritual–is an essential dynamic, I've always thought, in our pursuit to know the world, and our place within it. The pursuit of knowledge, of wisdom and, it is to be hoped, enlightenment. The attainment of the Ciceronian good life. My own attempt to say *I am an educated person,* and thus fulfill the blood contract of countless generations.

The distinction between identity and impulse can be made readily apparent through a conceit. Like a sailor, I always start cold–ice cold. I arrive at the dock of my imagination and go aboard, immerse myself in the objective rituals of preparation. What do I know about the voyage ahead? Is the rigging fit? Are the sheets trustworthy? Are my fuel tanks topped off? What do the charts say? Are the electronics operable? Whatever it takes to feel that sense of command you must feel, once you throw off the lines. That's identity for you, demanding definitions and certitude–Who am I? Where am I? What brings me here? Is this conceptual vessel seaworthy? Where to next?–before the writer/sailor feels confident enough to proceed.

Identity is not automatic; rather, for a free person it is an act of ritual and discipline and faith. Practically speaking, from a writer's point of view the answers aren't nearly as significant as the more existentially profound act of asking the questions, questions through which an identity is framed and constructed, and a purpose or goal suggested. Through such a process, form and content, the boat and the incipient voyage, become one.

Then, it pleases me to report, I cast off, raise the sails of impulse, and tack away into the dark expanse where anything can happen. This is how I think, this is how I write, and this, when life permits me, is how I live. Impulse catches the winds of possibility, which push the ship of identity into the unknown, where it can reinvent itself, or become more and more what it imagines itself to be. Call it a journey of discovery. You can also describe it as creative anarchy applied to the rational, scientific self, and thereby interpret the writer as mad inventor, inventing neither engines nor contraptions, but lives and worlds and the stories that reflect those lives, those worlds, yours and mine and the ones we've yet to set foot upon, familiar, exotic, or fantastic. I am an adult at the helm of my reality, yet in the most fundamental sense, I live the interior life of a six-year-old child: I spend many of my days making up things–imaginary friends, imaginary enemies, imaginary events, imaginary trouble, imaginary grace and redemption.

Why do this, why bother?–besides the fact that it is one of a thousand ways, and not so unpleasurable, to drift through a day, a year, a life. My reply, perhaps, is too simple, not exactly satisfying as an explanation: *because this is what human beings do.*

This is what is implied by the word *sentient*: by making a story or telling one, we awake to our selves, and our lives go forward. This is how human beings interact, how they struggle to identify themselves to one another, how they manage and compare and share the experience of existence, for friends and lovers, for strangers, and for the future.

Literature, Law, History, Biography, Journalism, the Cinema, all of the narrative modes of expression–aren't these nothing more, or less, than highly formalized genres of gossip? Who did what to whom, when, where, how and why, what does it all mean, and what was finally done about it? In one story, a wife takes a lover. In another, a man's obsession with a beast ends in disaster for his ship and crew. In another, a young boy runs away from home for a life-altering adventure on a river. Another young man fails his comrades-in-arms by running away from battle, afraid to die. We compare notes and decisions and circumstances and hearts; we recognize ourselves as traveling companions, the mutuality of our tenure on earth. *This is how it was for me,* we say, and then ask, *Tell me, sister, how was it for you?* Even in its most banal presentation, its most exploitative form, this divine gossip I call Literature is a vital act of community.

We imagine or investigate our way deeply into the chambers of another life, real or fantasized, with an acutely intense though not necessarily explicit purpose or instinct (other than the hypnotic, entertaining thrill of voyeurism). We imagine our way into each other's lives in order to experience empathy, to breach the possibility of compassion, to chance serious, sober encounters with the mystery of personality, so that eventually we might earn the right to say we *understand,* and, in understanding, to forgive what the world does to us. Or, conversely, in the fullness of understanding, to never, never forgive. Perhaps there is no greater human quest or spiritual dilemma than this.

Why do I write?

People must think this is an easy question to answer, since they ask it so readily of writers. I honestly think it is a strange question; to some extent, it begs a charade, solicits lies. Anais Nin thought the question equivalent to being asked why she breathed–meaning that, for some writers, once you inhale life, you are compelled to exhale language, and the act is not as conscious or deliberate as others take it to be. Certainly, writing is the way I've found to make my living. I appreciate it when other writers–the late Anthony Burgess, for instance–answer similarly.

Money, marketplace, profession. The game of commerce, sure. To be rich and famous, I could reply sophomorically, without undue shame over the thin vein of truth contained within such a response. I have realized lately–or perhaps the word *remembered* is more accurate here–that I cherish the rather transcendent moments when, like a small child, I am bathed in attention–make of that what you wish–but neither the desire for wealth or celebrity provide very illuminating insights into the issue of what motivates me to write.

I do know this: even though I've inferred otherwise, *I do not write to discover myself*. I think writers who declare such a motive are guilty of fraud, although it's probably true for anybody that you never really know the precise nature of how you feel about something until you write your way into it and through it. But, then what? I suppose what I'm reacting to here is the received truth that discovery is synonymous with change, progression, betterment of self: that writing has the capacity to lead you onward into some Buddhist state of wisdom and inner peace. How I wish that were true, but, in fact, the writing life is a paradox. A writer may indeed engrave a page with wisdom, serenity, beauty, and enlightenment, and yet in everyday life remain lodged in stupidity–unwise, tormented, unenlightened and ugly. While a writer's work might be angelic, his or her life might be simultaneously demonic; or, as is most often the case, merely human, as awkward and clumsy and flawed as anyone else's. You can–and perhaps *must*–manipulate the story and its characters with godlike authority, exerting a level of control you could never approach, not even as a tyrant, in your own life. Writers conjure their best, most focused and perfect selves and drag them to the page, but they can't walk off with those selves, back into reality, and have them make a difference.

Discovering oneself–that solipsistic exercise–isn't the point anyway. Discovering others, however, might be.

I've not led a mythic life, like a Hemingway or Conrad or Orwell, like a Dinesen or Woolf or Stein. Perhaps the age for that is over. Instead, despite a few lightening bolts sent my way, my life has been mostly commonplace, at least from my perspective, although I've battled against its ordinariness. If I could invent my own past, I'd surely fabricate something quite different than what I'm about to tell you. It's less true today than ever before in history, but the fact holds: the making, caretaking, and curating of Literature is still the province of the ruling class. But I'm afraid my tastes weren't passed on by way of a silver spoon. I have no tradition of genteel culture to impress you with, no drawing rooms or elite soirees. Do I envy such writers the privilege of their birth, their esthetic inheritance, their genetic codes. I confess at times I've stood outside the door to the clubhouse and felt famished, though not anymore. I suppose that whatever my affectations and pretentions are, others know them better than I do,but at least I understand they are lies, fictions, and more and more I find myself forced to accommodate the tension between the self that I invent and the selves that others invent for me.

No one's life is immune to perceptions; nevertheless, the facts of that life must be allowed the opportunity to speak for themselves. My story is very much the story of twentieth-century America, a story of immigration, of Ellis Island, of ethnic disadvantage, of having no alternative but to hammer a new world and a new life into existence; a story of upward mobility, of each generation sacrificing itself to provide a springboard for the next. The emblems of my tribe are pinochle and kielbasa and pickled mushrooms; old ladies with babushkas wrapped tight around their skulls, a cross of ashes smeared on their dry foreheads; the cidery, cabbage-and-coal smell of the Baltics; the sound of a language that was not English; the disillusioning climb away from poverty; outsiders grasping for the mainstream; children being educated irreversibly out of reach, beyond the world of their parents.

I know so little about my heritage. Visiting the Soviet Union as a college student in 1971, I was fascinated to learn that my family name, transcribed into the Cyrillic alphabet, consisted of only three letters, one for each syllable. Suddenly, my surname was as common-seeming and accessible as Fox or Jones. Years later, I was delighted to be told by a cousin that Shacochis, itself anglicized, wasn't really my family name at all, but a deception.

We were peasants, serfs, defined by occupation. During a czarist conscription drive in Lithuania, where my great-grandfather was a woodsman on a nobleman's vast estate, soldiers rapped on the door of his house where he lived with his wife and his sons. "Kapochus," an officer demanded, referring to his registry list, "you have four sons. We're taking them for the army."

"Wrong house," my great-grandfather lied. "I am not Kapochus [meaning, *the chopper*], I am Shacochus [meaning, *the branches*]. I have no sons." Actually, he had sent his boys to hide in the forest, then somehow booked passage on a steamer for the eldest, my paternal grandfather Martin, headed for America. Martin eventually made his way to the Lithuanian diaspora in northeastern Pennsylvania, where he worked for the railroad, then in the coal mines. My great-grandfather, the story goes, was murdered by Cossack poachers, who drove his own ax through his head. I am forever grateful to my ancestors for not coming to America earlier, and under more prosperous circumstances, thus bequeathing me some slight breathing room on the issues of race and class. I am amused when anyone, for all the wrong intentions, seeks to remind me that "my people" were responsible for enslaving someone else's people. That was hardly the case; in fact, the opposite was true, and eventually that truth would instill in me the courage to risk appropriating racial themes–one of the most volatile but crucial themes in American culture–for my fiction. I was willing to be held accountable for my own actions, but free from the burden of historical blame.

A final word on my Lithuanian legacy: this business of the family's situational name change continues to intrigue me. Is this why, I wonder, that in my fiction characters frequently have more than one name, depending on who's addressing them, and which of their selves, public or private, it most suits them to be in a particular context? I don't really have an answer for that.

I was born near Wilkes-Barre, in a town called West Pittston, on the banks of the Susquehanna River, in 1951–smack in the middle of the postwar baby boom. My parents were poor people who came of age, like so many of the parents of my generation, during the Great Depression, in an environment where they were looked down upon by their Anglo, Irish, and Italian neighbors. The stories of my parents' youth are rife with discrimination, and be assured that those stories had an effect on me.

As a teenager, my father earned his keep by caddying at the local golf course, learned the sport himself, and was talented enough to have joined his mentor, Art Wahl, on the pro tour, if the war hadn't intervened. I have also been told that, while working as a singing waiter at a resort in the Poconos, my father made an impression on Howard Hughes, who offered him a contract to make a movie with one of Hollywood's rising stars, a crooner named Frank Sinatra. My father says he turned Hughes down because he knew if he went to California he'd wind up ditching my mother. I don't know whether to believe that rationalization or not, but when I heard this story as a teenager myself, I made a mental note never to bypass an opportunity, never say no to a dream. Perhaps this is where my tenacity comes from: the do-or-die commitment that the writing life requires.

Eighteen months after my birth, my father concluded he was slowly walking down a dead-end street, uprooted his rapidly growing family–three boys and a girl on the way–and relocated us to the suburbs of Washington, D.C., where he entered into a thirty-year career as a quintessential bureaucrat, a civilian manager employed by the military, eventually retiring as the assistant director of the Bureau of Navy Personnel. In 1969, the year I enrolled in college, he went to Vietnam to reorganize the South Vietnamese Navy, and when I came home that summer from the university, with my hair down to my shoulders, wearing a T-shirt silkscreened with an angry red fist and the slogan *Strike!*, with the blood from my fellow students at Kent State running in the streets and the smoke of burned-out ROTC buildings fresh in my nostrils, we began to fight our own war, father and son, that I suppose, sadly, took too many years to end. His words that summer echo in my ears: "I wish I was dead, rather than to have spawned a son like you." Perhaps there is the beginning of the answer to why my esthetic universe rotates around the literature of political experience.

I grew up in that notorious realm known nationwide as "inside the Beltway," in a blue-collar neighborhood of saltbox tract housing. If there was a neighborhood theme, I suppose it would have to be white trash. Of course, first-generation Americans with ambition, as my parents were, thought of an environment like this as just another step up on the ladder into the mainstream.

I attended Catholic school–Our Lady of Good Counsel– where I was served the standard educational fare by nuns, who also taught me how to kneel and pray and cultivate a spinning sense of guilt, who schooled me in sin and confession and consequently, despite their intention, taught me how to lie. From the priests I learned Latin, in order to attend them as an altar boy; they also taught me how to box, but the first time I climbed into the ring I broke my best friend's nose and, horrified, I refused to do it anymore. My father, in fact, enjoyed telling his cronies I would grow up to join the priesthood. When it was clear I wasn't cut our for a life of religious devotion, I know he wanted me to be the world-class golfer he himself had once dreamed of being. I remember him telling me in high school to keep my hair well-groomed or I'd never get a job with the government. He denies it now, but what he didn't want me to be, what he actively tried to circumvent me from becoming, is what I became. A writer. Writing wasn't a life he could wrap his sight around, it had an amorphous shape, it was inhabited by far too many unstable characters and, to be fair, I suppose he saw the gamble as foolish, given the odds for success. Perhaps most important of all, there were no precedents for such a life within the family, no tradition of literacy or intellectual pursuit, no secular role models for such rarefied study.

The first question we writers are invariably asked is about when we started writing. As an antidote to so many absurd –in my opinion–responses from my colleagues, I have not been able to resist the glib answer: *I wrote my first novel in the womb,* I like to say, *but, the manuscript was misplaced during the confusion of the delivery.* The real answer, the private answer I've always told myself, is that I was a late bloomer, that I didn't begin writing in a serious, committed fashion, as if I saw my future in it, until I was twenty-six or twenty-seven, and even today when I approach a blank page, there's a desperate sense of newness to the activity, a provisional atmosphere, as though I'm trying something out for the first time, and there are no guarantees.

Still, in first and second grades, I used to write plays–one-act, one-man skits, I guess they should be called. Not only that, but I'd take them to class and perform them, which really begs the question: Are we born into this, we writers? Probably not. Words are basically another type of finger paint for children and, given the most minimal encouragement, all kids are creative. I suspect it is other things, darker things perhaps, than picking up a pen that really corner us into the box of our writing lives.

Something happened, I don't know what it was, and overnight my prepubescent career as a playwright went out the window. Something happened and I became pathologically self-conscious, secretive, and withdrawn. I could ease the frustration of this condition by telling myself I was shy–and my shyness, at least in my own mind, collapsed like a roof around me. It took twenty years to dig myself out from that ruination, but my sense of being an outsider continues to this day.

I became more comfortable with solitary pursuits, especially reading, that Siamese twin of writing. Comic books and travel books, anything that would sweep me away, adventure stories;

the books my mother read when she was a child, her entire collection of the Hardy Boys and the Bobbsey Twins. Whatever I felt the pressure to escape from, this was the trapdoor into safety. I was indeed one of those children who, ordered to bed, slipped under the covers with a flashlight and read for hours. I can't begin to say what actually took place, what changed me, whether it was sinister or a commonplace rite of passage, but I can speculate that I was beginning to realize how inadequately and carelessly we often listen to one another, how we struggle for each other's sincere attention. And how we can't seem to prevent ourselves from using what we hear when we do listen like a war club against each other, in judgment and in betrayal. And so I climbed down from my self-made stage of childhood, made books my best friends, and clammed up.

The ordinariness of these recollections almost suffocates me, yet I suppose if there is anything precious and lasting to me about those years in Pimmit Hills, it is that we were all young together, even my parents, and we were the naive and innocent family that we would never be again, once we crossed an invisible border and moved deeper into the suburbs – which I would later call a spiritual ghetto – to a middle-class neighborhood in McLean, where we left behind the fifties and marched, wide-eyed and eager, into the larger, more volatile and reckless world of the sixties.

What do I want to tell you about the sixties? *This:* that my adolescence was an adolescence of assassinations, riots, social upheaval, drugs, and war. Paradise destroyed. How could an American boy come of age during the 1960s and not go on to become a writer ensnared—even obsessed—by political experience, by power, by uncontrollable forces set into motion by reasonable men, what Robert Stone calls the "random promiscuity of events" that steamroll over unsuspecting lives? When you judge my generation, you must take this into account: that ours was an adolescence of assassinations; one by one, we watched our heroes' brains explode on TV and in our hearts we knew we would never really finish with the grief, nor with the rage. What planet were we on, we wondered, that could be so cruel?

I was one of those children whom America trained to crouch in school hallways and tuck up into a little ball, to protect myself in the event of a nuclear attack. I remember John Kennedy's radiance, who as a congressman attended our church, and as a president inaugurated Dulles Airport, and I was there in the crowd, idolizing him as only a ten-year-old boy could have. How my boyhood heart went out to him; he was the once-and-future king. My parents took me to the National Theater to see Richard Harris in *Camelot*, and maybe it was there, in the magical darkness, watching Lancelot betray Arthur, that I began to believe the true source of sadness was the beauty in our lives, the beauty of life itself. I never saw the Beatles. Instead, I saw Kennedy buried. I saw the riderless horse trot uncertainly down Pennsylvania Avenue. I saw two sailors fail to support each other and fall to the ground, weeping, in Arlington Cemetery. You can never comfort or repair the heart of a child who has seen such things.

I know now that my novel *Swimming in the Volcano* would never have been written were it not for John Kennedy and his vision of the Peace Corps, his belief in the altruism and the fundamental goodness of Americans. I would also like to remind you that the protagonist in my novel, Mitchell Wilson, quotes Henry Adams on General Robert E. Lee: "Sometimes it's the good men among us who do the most harm in the world."

A year after J.F.K. was laid to rest, for the first time in my life I saw a man with long hair: it was Bobby Kennedy, who occasionally chaperoned the youth dances at our church. I had seen him several times before, but this night, dressed in white pants and white shirt, with his hair below his ears, he looked like an archangel; he looked like one of the actors who had walked off the stage at the National Theater and come to participate in our lives.

Today I know all the dirt about the Kennedys, but I don't see how that changes anything. As a boy I lived among the gods: however romantic, this is one of the central facts of my universe.

Even as a middle-aged man, I insist, with irrational stubbornness, on having my heroes, and am sourly disappointed–and yet I suppose relieved–when they decline to accept the status I have assigned them.

Where do a writer's sensibilities come from? All I know is that in my own consciousness, my past resides like a chiaroscuro painting; much of the canvas sunk in darkness; scattered shafts of brilliant light that penetrate to the bone. Those shadowed peripheries, the subconsciousness: that's where the writing life really rumbles and shakes with pent-up energy.

In the promising spring of 1968, I was a love-struck, surf-crazed sixteen-year-old junior in high school, talking foolishly about marriage with a girl who was a senior. She was a feature writer for the school newspaper; I was the sports editor, and the following year I would be promoted to managing editor. That newspaper–*The McLean High School Highlander*–had a major impact on my life, as did *The Washington Post*, which I read every morning with my breakfast before walking to school. *The Highlander* was by no means your average high school newspaper. We reported on the Pentagon demonstrations, the anti-war marches, we attended government press conferences, we editorialized about Vietnam and civil rights and the sexual revolution; we engaged fully with the world around us, which was enormously big but accessible as long as we cared to reach out to it. Publicists knew to call us if they wanted the fanfare to reach directly to the boomers. I interviewed (don't laugh) Wayne Newton, Twiggy. Stanley Kubrick and Arthur C. Clarke invited us, six months before it would be released, to a special screening of their movie *2001: A Space Odyssey*, then asked for our opinions and insights. It was heady stuff.

But that spring we saw Washington burning. A carload of us had driven down south to Lexington, and it was there that we heard the news: Martin Luther King had been shot and killed in Memphis. I remember standing in a phone booth on Route 29, talking to my mother in McLean. She was hysterical; off in the direction of the city, she could see smoke rising above the trees, and she feared for our safe return. We drove numbly straight to Rosslyn, on the Virginia side of the Potomac, overlooking Washington. There were tanks and soldiers on Key Bridge. Black clouds of smoke with hearts of orange fire mushroomed into the sky above downtown. Occasionally we could hear the crack of gunfire echoing across the river, and we stood mutely, with wordless vertigo, wondering what was happening to our world, wondering who could ever explain this to us, or explain in what ways our lives were being altered forever, and how we'd ever adapt, and who or what could ever be relied upon to ensure our happiness.

That June of '68, I worked for a lawn-care outfit run by some older friends of mine–college-age entrepreneurs who were too clever and ambitious and free to bother with any education higher than the one they were giving themselves. One morning, my mother came down the steps in a blue house robe to where I lay sleeping in my basement bedroom. When I felt her hand on my shoulder, my first thought was that I had overslept for work, that my ride was outside waiting, but then I heard the tears in my mother's voice before I saw them in her eyes. "Bob, get up," she said, barely able to whisper. "Bobby's been shot." I knew immediately whom she meant. I pulled on a pair of shorts and turned on the TV. There was the last golden hero of my youth, lying on the floor of a hotel kitchen in Los Angeles, his head haloed in blood, staring up into the startling unexpectedness of eternity. I remember saying out loud, again and again, "That's it, that's it," and finally, "I hate America."

One more scene from that summer. There's a party; it's a farewell party for one of the guys I work with, Charlie. Charlie's been drafted, he's being shipped to Vietnam. We were all drunk and Charlie, usually a quiet, sharp-eyed twenty-year-old, was very drunk, stumbling around, laughing like a hyena. Toward the end of the evening, when it was time for us all to disperse, Charlie was sobbing out of control and he wouldn't walk. His best friend,

I forget his name but he was a huge and brawny fellow, propped Charlie up against the side of his '57 Chevy, cocked back his right arm, and punched Charlie's lights out. I had seen dead people before but I had never seen this, someone knocked unconscious and dropped like a log. Charlie hit the ground with a sickening thud, his head bouncing, and as I watched his friend pick him up and sling Charlie's deadweight over his shoulder and carry him away, nothing was ever more clear to me than this: that Charlie was lost to us, that Charlie wasn't ever going to make it back home again, and six months later when I was told that a mortar round had landed right in Charlie's lap as he sat in his bunker in Southeast Asia and blew him to bits, I wasn't shocked or surprised because I felt I had already seen him die, I had been holding the image of his death in my mind for all those months.

I harbor no sense of nostalgia about the sixties, only an abiding sorrow and vestigial weariness. Whenever I needed a reprieve from the turmoil and chaos of those times, I fled to the only sanctuary I knew of, the beach.

Beaches have always been a traditional venue for outcasts and rebels, an ecology where you could pantomime the rites of manhood and yet go right ahead and reject the implications in favor of a higher order of meaning, if you happened to know of one. At the age of seventeen, against my father's injunction. I was tantalized off the North American continent by a photograph I had seen in the pages of *Surfer* magazine, a publication that championed a counterculture subcult for loners, and developed a new language, and a new style of writing about the intensity of experience. I'm not kidding about this: *Surfer* magazine, the New Journalists like Tom Wolfe, and the black humorists like J.P. Donleavy, John Barth, and Thomas Pynchon made the first, and most enduring, impression on those sensibilities that I would follow into the writing life. Sorry, neither Henry James nor Hemingway were on my radar screen.

There were no waves to ride in St. Thomas, where the pretty

picture in the magazine had been snapped. So, I hitched a ride in a motorboat across the channel to the island of St. John. It is in the natural order of things that boys make asses out of themselves as they try to become the heroes of their own lives–though they have no monopoly on the behavior–and beaches are the perfect backdrops for such posturing.

You meet all manner of eccentrics on the shores and summits of the Caribbean, and in some ways they are the true treasures of the islands. In a tent down the path from mine camped a lone middle-aged man, a shoe designer from Atlanta, and I thought of him as a guy with no ability to exploit the available resources. He was peculiar but by no means contemptible, and even by my style-conscious standards he deserved peripheral curiosity.

One night I strolled over to his campsite, attracted by his radio–the only artificially created sound to be heard issuing from the darkness–and the excitement of its broadcast: Momentarily men were going to land on the moon, a lemony wafer ascending through the palms. We stared at the radio as the lunar module began its descent, and the voice of a woman shouted out of the night from a campsite nearby: "Turn that goddamn thing off!"

I yelled back that men were about to set foot on the moon, and suggested a place she herself should go.

"Moon, schmoon," she complained. "Turn off that noise."

Against my protest, the man from Atlanta smiled wistfully, shrugged, and obeyed her. "She's got a point," he said. Moonlight and moonshadow filtered down around us through the black lace of vegetation over our heads. I asked him to explain the point he had just conceded. "Esthetics before information, or you'll never have any good use for information."

He continued, "Unless you plan on being Tarzan when you grow up, esthetics are what you came here to develop, even if you don't know it yet." Then he left me without another word to walk out from under the canopy of trees and eyeball the silent violation of the moon.

Four years later, after an asphyxiating university education crammed with sterile facts and figures, I returned to the Caribbean to spend a year with native fishermen, relearning how to learn. The gentleman from Atlanta had risen in my opinion to the stature of a Yaqui brujo—sorcerer. Considering who I was at the time, it's probably for the best that I received this wisdom not from some native shaman, but from a fellow who designed footwear and lived in the suburbs.

But where did a white middle-class kid from the suburbs go in 1973 to develop an abiding sense of community, family, tolerance, and generosity, those values that never truly stuck to me, growing up in the spiritual ghetto of McLean? All I know is that at the age of twenty-two, I wanted out. "Love it or leave it" was still a potent message in American society. Nixon had been reelected, the war was still on, Watergate had yet to unscroll its ugliness, and I did indeed not love my country; the only medicine I knew for this condition, instinctively, was to leave. And so I did. I was gone for three years and came back cured, more or less.

As destiny would have it, I alighted on the island of Providencia in San Andrés, an off-the-map archipelago and budding Colombian resort, for a year, rented a house on the beach in a village called Old Town, and became the neighbor and friend of a man named Raimundo Lung. Robertson Davies once wrote that a man in his youth has several fathers, and his biological one isn't necessarily the most significant. I had three: the one who fathered my body; a professor in Missouri—William Peden is his name—who fathered my passion to be a writer; and Mundo, the third and most adroit, a penniless black spearfisherman, the father of my spiritual point of view, who taught me how to persevere in the face of hardship and never be afraid of life.

Mundo's pedagogy was basic: watch and learn. He rarely gave instructions or advice or reproach, except when danger was imminent. He allowed me my mistakes, and I accepted his affectionate bemusement with my awkwardness. Occasionally he would say, about something good or bad, wrong or right: *That is the black man's way.* Occasionally, I would say the same thing about whites, but generally the issue of race was so mundane and pointless that we never discussed it except as one of God's weird jokes, of which there were plenty.

One thing about Mundo: he was, and is, clairvoyant. Years later, as a student at the Iowa Writers' Workshop, I was compelled to write about this power of his, fictionalizing the truth of events I was unable to comprehend, and although I had crafted an alter ego for myself, I was unable to give Mundo any other name—or reality—but his own. In life, Mundo had always been larger than life. The same goes for duppy-haunted Providencia, rubbing itself so intimately against nature. The islands have always played *Twilight Zone* tricks on me, suggesting, among other things, that there were moments of mysticism inherent in the human act of expression, including the act of writing, moments of prophecy, moments of hyperlucidity, moments that would reach out to tear a souvenir off the coattails of the future. Where does an imagination come from? I found myself asking on Providencia, but the island always answered back with a riddle—*Where does reality come from?*—and a biblical reproach: In the beginning was the Word. It's the language, dummy. The narrative might be domestic or political, but there was no other link between real events and the imagination but language and nature.

Mistah Bob? I hear Mundo's wife, Concha, saying to me. *Listen, when we are bairn we are each given a destiny, not so?*

I want to answer petulantly, wearily, cynically: *I know I know I know.* But I don't, really.

Or I want to say, *Deaths, yes. Destinies, no. Destinies you wrestle with, until they shake you off.*

Here is the revelation that Providencia left me with: time and chronology are two different animals; the latter tame, a beast of burden; the former wild, unruly, popping in and out of holes, coming at you from all directions, everywhere at once.

Out of money and health, I took my leave of Providencia, got well, took a job as a chauffeur in Europe, then joined the

Peace Corps as my ticket back to the Caribbean, where I served as an agricultural journalist on the islands of St. Vincent, Barbados, and St. Kitts. By this time–1976–I had fallen in love with the woman who would become my wife, and my island fever began to undergo a metamorphosis into an obsession with writing. These twin passions swept me off to another direction. I laugh to think of the reasons why I didn't dedicate myself to writing earlier in my life. Spike Lee once said that when he was growing up, he spent a lot of time in movie theaters, but he had a better idea about where babies came from than where movies came from. Spike didn't find out until he went to college. It was the same for me with books, and I was afraid to throw myself into an apparently formless, unstructured life that depended on self-discipline, which I had very little of. No office, no boss, no paycheck. The more real fears I harbored were that I wasn't smart enough, and that I was a person without a very useful array of obsessions. My obsessions were not intellectual, but emotional and political, and I felt I couldn't sustain or manipulate them in a productive way. I came to learn, however, that I only take myself seriously when I write. I write to keep myself educated and when I don't write, I feel myself–and my intelligence–rapidly fading into oblivion, where I'm perfectly content to be the ne'er-do-well my parents were once so concerned I would become.

I write because I hold the conviction, smarmy as it might seem, that we must give back to that from which we take. Take a penny, leave a penny. What I've most taken from in my life is the banquet table of literature. What most fulfills my sense of worth are my own attempts to contribute to this timeless feast, to keep the food replenished and fresh, perhaps introduce an unfamiliar recipe, or a variation on one of the favorites. *There are no old myths,* the writer Jim Harrison once said, *only new people.*

But the foremost reason I write might at first strike you as petty. I write for revenge–that time-honored but somewhat cliched motivation. Living well isn't the best revenge, I can tell you from experience. Writing well, on the other hand, is.

Revenge against apathy, against those who are not interested in listening to the voices that surround them–wife, husband, brother, daughter, father, friend or nameless traveler.

Revenge against the bullets of assassins, against the wild forces that trample the earth, against the terror and tragedy that is in every life.

Revenge against the Devil and, pardon the blasphemy, revenge against God, for slaughtering us in the crossfire of their eternal quarrel.

Why do I write? Because I know my children's children, and your children's children, would like to hear a story before they go to sleep, and I'd like to tell them one so that when they finally close their eyes, the story will melt into a dream, and the dream will fill the emptiness, the loneliness, and leave them with a magnificent burning image of desire to be alive, and who can say with certainty, Which is the story? Which is the dream? And which is life? I want to tell my stories with the franticness of a parent whose child is dying, as if the story can keep the child alive until help arrives.

I write for revenge against silence, revenge against the endless silence that seems to erupt, right beyond the tips of humanity's fingers, into infinity; revenge against the silence into which we fall.

Against that silence, we move, we create. We breathe. Exhale.

Fort Lauderdale, Florida, 1994

BOB SHACOCHIS has published two collections of short stories, *Easy in the Islands,* which won the National Book Award, and *The Next New World;* a novel, *Swimming in the Volcano,* a 1993 National Book Award finalist; and *Domesticity,* a collection of essays. He is a contributing editor to *Harper's* and *Outside* magazines.

Hotaling's News Agency, New York City

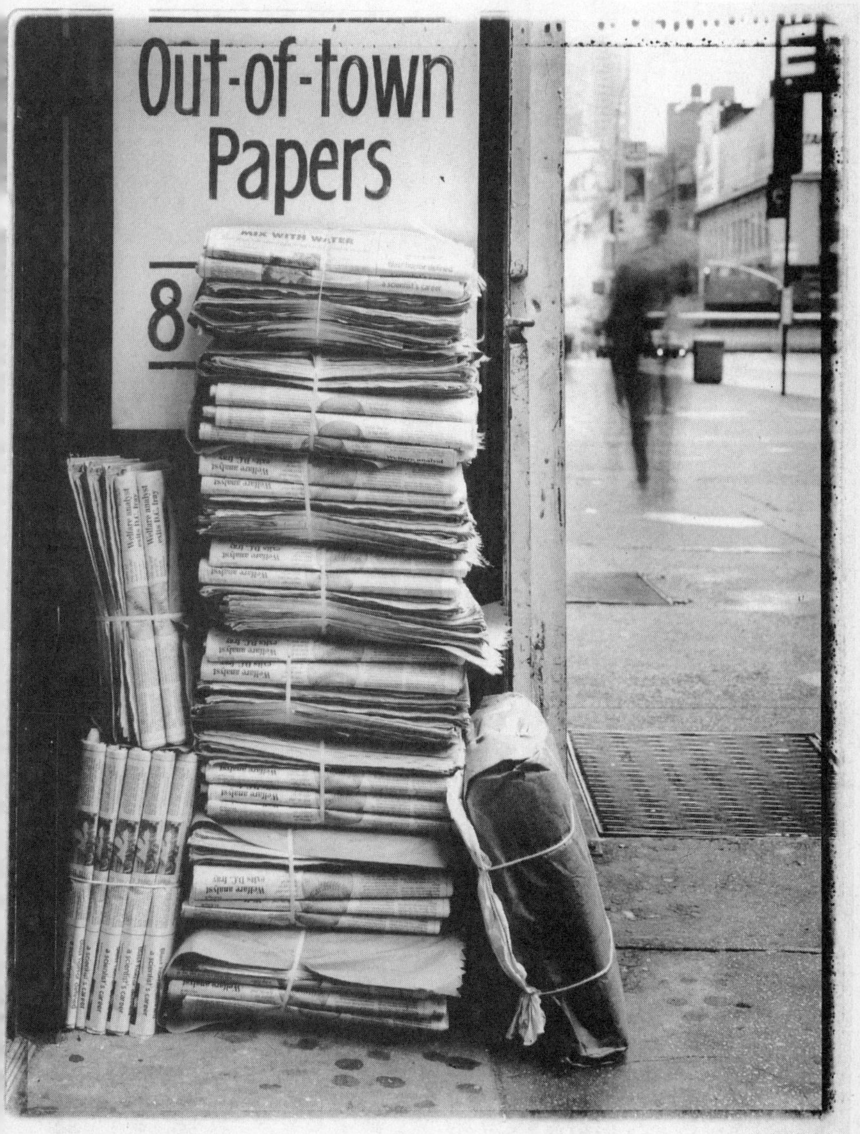
Out-of-town
Papers

From Beirut to Jerusalem to Washington

Thomas L. Friedman

To the casual observer it looks as though I was a journalist who wrote a book. End of story. It has been done a thousand times before and will be done a thousand times more. Actually, I have had what I consider to be at least four distinctly different writing-reporting experiences in my career, each of which imparted to me some very important and distinctly different lessons.

I break my own writing life into four parts, each of which happens to correspond to different geographical locations in which I have lived as a reporter and writer. In the beginning there was Beirut, then Jerusalem, then writing a book in between Jerusalem and Washington, and finally working as a reporter in Washington.

The most important thing Beirut teaches you, or maybe forces you to learn as a journalist, is how to operate in a city without officials. It is a particularly stark lesson for anyone who comes from Washington, which is a city in which there are only officials! In Beirut there are none. There are no officials who count and no government to speak of. That is why I entitled the chapter in my book about reporting from Beirut: "Beirut, City of Versions." As my colleague the late Bill Farrell once observed, "There is no truth in Beirut, only versions."

I once described to someone what it is like to be a reporter in Beirut. It's as if you are standing there watching this white light of truth coming at you. But before it hits you it is refracted through this prism of Lebanese factions and fiefs and religious groups, so that before it reaches your eyes it is splayed out in fifteen different directions. Your challenge as a reporter is to grab a little bit of the blue band, and a little bit of the red band, and a little bit of the green band, and try to paint as close a picture of reality as you possibly can. It's like being in a dark tunnel, aided only by a single candle looking for the light at the other end. And you see a light and chase it only to discover that it is someone else also with a candle, also looking for the light at the other end.

This situation had its advantages and disadvantages. The upside was that what made Beirut such an exciting place to be as a reporter is that you could get to see things there that you would not be able to see in virtually any other reporting environment. There were no police sawhorses in Beirut to separate the reporters from the actors. There was no precinct spokesman who said, "I'm sorry, you can't go down that road, but I'll tell you what's happened." In Beirut, you could get into your car and drive as far as your courage or your gas tank would take you. That meant some reporters not only drove right into the battle but drove through the battle and out the other side. There was literally nothing to stop you. As a result, you got to see scenes, you got to see emotions, you got to see battles at a proximity which you could not imagine on any other story. The only thing I can compare it to is being at a theater where you could actually go up on stage in the middle of play and talk to the actors while they were reciting their lines.

"So, tell me, Hamlet, what's this problem you have with your stepfather?"

For a reporter or a writer that is the ultimate high. It really enabled me to enlarge myself as a writer very early in my career by exposing me to an unusually broad range of emotions and bizarre encounters from one end of the human spectrum to the other. Having to, and being able to, describe some of the incredible scenes that cross your path on any given day in Beirut stretches your writing muscles like a literary aerobic.

The downside of that kind of environment is that because nothing is official everything is official. At some level, everybody's story becomes equally true, everyone's version equally valid. A reporter could get up in the morning, sit down at his typewriter and write, "Fifteen Christians were massacred on the Green Line today by thirty Shiite Moslems."

Who can check? I'm not going to go down to the Green Line and check. The police are not going to go down to the Green Line and check. It is an exaggerated example, to be sure, but in a paradoxical way such an environment really teaches you a writer's discipline. As a reporter you had to go that extra mile yourself to confirm, or try to confirm, what was true and what was false. You did not have the luxury of being able to just pick up the phone and say: "O.K., Mr. Spokesman, what's true and what's not?" You had to report every story ten times and from ten different angles if you wanted to make sure that it was correct. For the best reporters this imposed a great burden. For the worst reporters it really gave them free rein. And that's why we saw some remarkable excesses in reporting from Beirut during the summer of 1982. One reporter for a major American network reported one day that six square blocks of West Beirut were "dust and rubble."

Six square blocks? Do you know how big six square blocks is? I mean there was a lot of dust and a lot of rubble there. But it wasn't six square blocks, except on the Green Line where fighting had been going on for years. But who could check?

What often happened as a result of this freewheeling reporting environment was that because we as reporters are so trained to rely on sources some reporters almost invented sources or spokesmen where none existed. There was a wire service in Beirut that ran a story one day which it attributed to "leftist" sources: "According to leftist sources..."

"What is a leftist source?" I wondered. Is that people who are left-handed?" In West Beirut everyone is a leftist source. That's like quoting "Jewish sources" in Israel. But people used the term to put a ring of authenticity into their reporting where none naturally existed.

The second thing that Beirut really taught me as a journalist and as a writer was to appreciate the moment. As I noted in my book, some of my colleagues came to Beirut and could not leave because they became hooked on their own adrenaline and on the daily bang-bang that gets you on the front page or the evening news. I was not immune to that myself. When I think back on Beirut now, I barely remember the close calls or the adrenaline highs. Instead, I always come back to certain "moments"–those remarkable human encounters I got to witness that taught me more about people and what they are made of than anything in the previous twenty-five years of my life. I got to see with my own eyes the boundaries of men's compassion alongside their unfathomable brutality, their ingenuity alongside astounding folly, and their insanity alongside their infinite ability to endure.

Of course for the Lebanese who starred in the moments of my memory, there was no thrill, only the numbing routine of survival, punctuated by an occasional moment of levity. I never forgot that my moments were usually their nightmares. Gerald Butt, then the BBC correspondent in Beirut, told me a story that happened toward the end of the summer of '82 that really brought this home to me. A group of Lebanese doctors and nurses had decided to organize a protest march across the Green Line from West Beirut to East Beirut, to draw world attention to the Israeli siege, which had caused a shortage of medical supplies in West Beirut. The march took place at the Galerie Sama'an crossing point between East and West, a barren mile-long stretch of road flanked by half-destroyed apartment buildings purged of all life except snipers.

"At the time, I really didn't think about it being dangerous," Butt later recalled. "I just thought, well, here's a story that

I should be covering, so I joined the march. There were about twenty doctors and nurses, and someone at the front carried a Red Cross flag. When we got about halfway across the Green Line, I looked around and saw that there was no cover anywhere. We were in the middle of the Green Line! There was shelling nearby, snipers all around, and I was walking with these doctors. I just said to myself, 'What am I doing here?' And then I turned to look back and I saw a Lebanese man just a few meters behind us, and he was leading a white horse. A white horse! It looked like a racehorse.... He must have heard that there was going to be a march across the Green Line and he wanted to use us for cover to get his horse out of West Beirut. He probably couldn't feed it because of the shortage of food and water. It was so surreal. These doctors, and the Red Cross flag and the shelling and this man tagging along with his white racehorse."

It is for such moments that a reporter is drawn to Beirut, and stays there long after good sense tells him he should leave. The front-page stories, the six-column headlines over your byline, those were all a great thrill at the time. But they don't last, only the moments do.

Whenever I try to explain this irrational tug of Beirut, I am reminded of that joke that Woody Allen tells at the end of *Annie Hall.* A guy goes to his doctor and says, "Doctor, doctor, I have got a terrible problem, my brother thinks he is a chicken." And the doctor says, "That's crazy, just tell him he's not a chicken." The guy says, "I can't. I need the eggs."

I kept coming back to Beirut because I needed the eggs. And the eggs were the moments.

An appreciation for those moments which bring a story alive and convey certain universal truths may be the most important lesson any writer could ever learn. There is reporting, there is good reporting, and then there is great reporting. What distinguishes one from the other? In my opinion, "good reporting" is a combination of good analysis of an event and good anecdotes–

that is, good picturesque moments that really bring the analysis alive. It can be something as simple as the way an official gestured with his hand to something as complicated as a personal family saga. But it is that moment that brings your analysis alive to the reader in a pungent way and in a way in which he or she can really relate to the analytical point you are trying to make. A story that is only anecdotal is like a series of pictures without any text. A story that is only analytical is like a text without any pictures.

As a reporter in Beirut you could write on any given day that the mood in the city had turned very pessimistic. Or you could try a different approach. My ultimate political source in Beirut was a glassmaker. He was a Lebanese who probably had not even finished high school. He had never heard of George Gallup. But Riyad, as he was called, knew one thing. He knew that when people were ordering glass it meant that they were confident about the future, and confident that a new round of fighting was not about to explode that would shatter their windows. Very simple. When people were upbeat and confident, everyone was replacing windows and business for Riyad boomed. When people felt that the political situation was about to deteriorate or continue to be bad they replaced their broken windows with plastic sandwich wrap and business for Riyad was awful. He became, like the proverbial Maytag repairman, the loneliest man in town. So as a reporter you could say to the reader flat out: People in Beirut are pessimistic. Or you could say that people are pessimistic and now let me tell you about the visit I had last week with my friend Riyad.

This approach requires several things from the writer. First, it means understanding that you constantly need to have your ear to the ground–talking to everyone from presidents to grocers–to have a feel for where the "Story" with a capital *S* is at all times. Second, you constantly have to be on the lookout for the telling anecdote or gesture–and it could come anytime, anywhere–that would illuminate that story. And third, through a process of trial and error, you constantly have to be seeking out these people in whatever country you happen to be living in who are original thinkers. An original thinker is someone who thinks for himself, never gets caught up in the conventional wisdom, and has that ability to articulate the universal truths contained in your anecdotes as well as to bring your own analysis to a higher level. This is how I work as a reporter. I am constantly interacting with my environment, trying to monitor the mood and keep my pulse on where and what the story is, and, at the same time, constantly bringing my anecdotes and intuitions on a platter to the best minds I can find to help me figure out just what they mean.

There is a story I tell in my book about going to the Bar Mitzvah of an Israeli cousin of mine and being surprised at the fact that he ordered pork chops for lunch at the meal following the ceremony. I just tucked that away and then as soon as I got back to Jerusalem I called one of my original-thinking sources on religious matters, and related the story to him. Together my source and I would figure out the story's meaning like a puzzle. Sometimes these conversations would go on over several days until I, or we, was satisfied that we had gotten to the bottom of it. The best compliment I ever get from a source is when he or she says to me after one of these sessions: "You know, that was fun. I had not really articulated any of these things in this way until you forced me to think about it." I never go to an analytical source looking for "a quote." I always come carrying some problem, scene, encounter, or mystery and ask for help understanding it. I have found that if you come to these sessions with good questions and good anecdotes, you will take away good insights. Come empty, leave empty.

The third thing that Beirut taught me as a reporter, paradoxically really, is to appreciate not only the moments, but, just as importantly, the silence. Sometimes a journalist was kidnapped there and someone would say. "Why him? How could they have kidnapped *him*? Why, he knew everybody in town."

Well, he may have known everybody who made it their business to have contact with journalists, but that was it. Beirut taught me how little you can really know about the place where you are living. Take for example February 1984. During that month the Shiites of West Beirut mounted a revolution in the streets that took practically everyone in the city by surprise. One day after the revolt had finished, my wife and I were eating lunch at the Commodore Hotel, the clubhouse for all Western journalists. This wild-eyed Shiite gunman came into the hotel, stalked through the lobby, and went straight into the bar. The bartender had been expecting him, and had hid all the liquor bottles under the bar and had built a pyramid of Pepsi cans where the Johnny Walker once stood. But this Shiite militiaman wasn't fooled. He swept the bartender aside, went behind the bar, and methodically broke every bottle and glass in the house with the butt of his rifle.

As I watched him I kept thinking that this guy was probably one of my neighbors. It pointed out how little I really knew about the subterranean emotions that were coursing under Beirut. In fact, I left Beirut with a variation of Groucho Marx's line that any club that would have me as a member, I didn't want to join. Official source who will talk to me, I don't want to speak to. Those who talk to journalists don't really know what's happening. The people who are out kidnapping journalists, or blowing up marine headquarters, don't give interviews to *Time* magazine. They just do it. They don't go to the Commodore Hotel bar and sidle up and say: "Hey, Friedman, guess what I just blew up!"

I also learned to appreciate the silence by occasionally discovering that the real story was in what was not being said, rather than in what was being said. Take for instance the day the marines' headquarters in Beirut were blown up—October 23, 1983. It was 6:20 A.M. and my wife, Ann, and I were awakened by an explosion that literally wiggled our whole apartment house, despite the fact that the blast was actually ten miles away. As we drove out of our neighborhood to see what it was, there was a small group of Lebanese men playing tennis at the local clay court club. Two hundred forty-one Americans had just been blown up, and they were playing tennis. They didn't know where the explosion had happened, of course. But the ground, the court, the very clay under their feet, must have shaken them to the core. And later in the day, when everyone knew what had happened, people were still playing tennis. That became a telling incident for me about the real attitudes toward the Americans in Lebanon. The Lebanese loved the marines when they came, supposedly to protect them from anarchy. But when the Lebanese discovered that the marines could not even protect themselves, they came to look upon them with disdain. I could have interviewed hundreds of people, and sooner or later that sentiment would have been expressed. Or, I could have done what I did in this case–just listened to their silence.

The last thing Beirut really taught me was a tremendous respect for the street and the wisdom of the street. Working in a city with no officials, you learn to depend on your grocer, your maid, and your local butcher as your political sources. When no one is the government, everyone is the government. When no one is an official source, everyone is an official source. Nine times out of ten, the way I would go about writing a story in Beirut was not to seek out some "Western diplomat" or unnamed official. Rather, I would draw up a list of all the nurses, grocers, and bankers I knew–the people who interacted with society at large –and talk to them one by one. My best sources in Beirut were bankers. Because bankers become psychoanalysts in their own way by observing what people do with their most valued assets. I would also interview nurses, and grocery store owners, and even proverbial taxi drivers. Once I had a sense of what the street felt like, what the street was saying, I had a sense of the limits of politics. It didn't matter what President Amine Gemayel declared was going on, or what he was intending to do or not do.

I'll never forget one day in the early 1980s when I was having lunch with Elie Salem, Lebanon's foreign minister. It was a fancy lunch in East Beirut, with twelve senior foreign correspondents in attendance. Salem was going on and on, telling us about the political situation, how everything was going to improve, how Lebanon really was not locked in civil war. Seated directly across from him, I asked him about what he thought were the political implications of the mood in the street. Moslem West Beirut was under curfew at the time and Christian East Beirut, where Salem lived, wasn't. And if you lived in West Beirut, as I did, you could feel the anger there just welling up in the streets. I said to him, "Mr. Minister, do you realize the pressures people feel?" And then I described to him what my maid and grocer had all been saying to me.

I don't remember his answer, but he turned to his secretary, who was seated at the far end of the table, and said to her in Arabic, "I guess you were right." It was clear that his secretary had been telling him just what I had said.

Jerusalem was a totally different assignment for me. The first thing I had to come to terms with there was what exactly does it mean for a writer to be "objective."

It wasn't an accident that it was in Jerusalem where I felt this question most acutely, because I was the first Jewish reporter *The New York Times* ever assigned to full-time Jerusalem. The *Times* had for many years had an unwritten rule that said you don't send a Jew to Israel because people will say that he or she is not objective—can't possibly be objective—no matter how or what they write.

Most journalism textbooks will advise you that if you want to get the most objective journalist possible for the Middle East find a Gentile from Wyoming who has never met an Arab or Jew in his life. To that I say, nonsense. Objectivity should not be synonymous with ignorance.

Objectivity is a tension, a tension between two conflicting impulses: understanding and disinterest. I can't possibly write a fair story, an insightful story, an honest story unless I get close enough to my subjects to understand what makes them tick. I can't possibly write a fair story about Israelis or Palestinians unless I become knowledgeable about their history, and also get close enough to them as individuals so that I am almost inside their heads, looking at the world as they do. Because without that kind of deep understanding–understanding that borders on sympathy–I can't possibly be fair.

At the same time, I have to maintain a certain distance and level of disinterest, because if I don't, I will understand only them. A reporter is never going to get it perfectly balanced in every story of every book. Sometimes you may be a little too distant, at other times a little too understanding. But you've got to feel that tension all the time. Understanding without disinterest lapses into commitment, and disinterest without understanding lapses into banality. So whenever anyone asked me how I as a Jew could be "objective," my answer was always that objectivity is not something that you are born with. It is a state of mind that you have to aspire to and anyone–Christian, Muslim, or Jew–can aspire to it. Judge me on what I write, not on my birth certificate.

Another thing that Jerusalem teaches you is a real appreciation for words and exactitude. I often say that Jerusalem is the only assignment where they will kill a reporter for a conjunction. As a *New York Times* reporter in particular, you work there under a tremendous spotlight. It is like no other reporting assignment as the extent to which your copy is scrutinized and psychoanalyzed by readers. "Why did you put a 'but' there and not a comma? Why did you put a comma there and not a semicolon? What does that say about you? What does that say about your mother or your attitude toward Judaism?" These are all questions that were hurled at me at one time or another, and they taught me to weigh my words very carefully.

I happened to arrive in Jerusalem in September 1984, around the time that the first national unity government was being formed, but I was on vacation the day the new cabinet was actually announced. So my Israeli assistant, Moshe Brilliant, who was in his early seventies, ended up reporting and filing the story. The cabinet announcement broke late at night so Moshe had to dictate the story to *The New York Times* over a scratchy phone line. He also had to dictate the cabinet list. Speaking into the phone he began at the top and went right down: "Prime Minister, from the Labor Party, Shimon Peres; Vice Prime Minister and Foreign Minister, from the Lijud Party, Yitzhak Shamir." When he got to Dr. Joseph Burg, a very learned Orthodox politician, he said: "Dr. Joseph Burg, veteran National Religious Party leader, Minister of Religious Affairs." The person on the other end of the phone heard, "Bedouin National Religious Party leader," not "veteran." So, *The New York Times* comes out at 11:00 P.M., the cabinet list is there, and it says Joseph Burg, Bedouin National Religious Party Leader. It is hard to imagine a bigger mistake. No sooner was the paper out than someone called Dr. Burg in Israel and someone from Israel called *The New York Times* and, I'm told, the story was corrected in time before the next edition.

As much as I thought that I had learned every lesson I possibly could as a writer in Jerusalem–to weigh my words very, very carefully, and think about every comma and conjunction–when I wrote my book, I discovered I hadn't learned anything at all. It amazed me that with all my experience as a reporter I could write a book that would produce reactions that I totally didn't anticipate, and reactions that were so widely divergent. It has fascinated me to see how, with a book as opposed to a newspaper story, readers take away from it what they bring to it.

I received a letter calling me a "self-hating Jew," and another praising my book as a compelling saga. Same book, same mailbag, same day. Both letters from Jews. I eventually realized that this book has become a sort of out-of-body experience. I wrote it and now it's out there, and it seems to have taken on a life and persona all its own. And it's almost no longer mine in a way. That's both humbling and frustrating.

The transition from Beirut to Jerusalem to book to Washington is a strange one indeed, particularly the leap from foreign reporting in the Middle East to diplomatic reporting in Washington. What I always tell people is that I feel as though I have gone from covering a street to covering a hall, and from covering a drama unfolding before my eyes to covering a policy that is invisible. You can't say, "I met the policy today. She wept on my shoulder," or "I saw the policy bleeding today at the C-Street entrance to the State Department."

When people ask me what I do for a living, I like to tell them that I cover people who watch CNN. I have gone from being able to smell the street in my own nostrils to being three steps removed, and that can be enormously frustrating for a writer who depends on anecdote and texture to bring his analysis alive. It kills me when I meet people in Washington who will say to me, "Oh, I loved your reporting from Jerusalem." And then they will say, "What are you doing now?" People just don't remember stories based on "Administration sources said today."

Another frustration I find about working in Washington, particularly as the diplomatic correspondent, is that your world shrinks to twelve people. When I was in Jerusalem or Beirut and some government spokesman would say, "Well, it's not like that in Gaza or Sidon." I could just answer back, "Yeh, well I was just in Gaza and let me tell you what it is like." I would go for months in both cities without talking to anyone resembling an official. You can't do that in Washington, because here there are only officials. And here, it doesn't really matter what you may think reality is out there. What matter is how the top officials in the government see it, since they are the ones creating the invisible policy that we cover. As a reporter you always have to walk that tightrope between maintaining access to the twelve or so officials who really know what is going on and, at the same time, not getting so close to them that you can't stand back and kick them in the shins when you have to.

I am still trying to figure out how you bring Washington alive. How do bring an arms control story alive? One of the things that I have tried to bring to my reporting in Washington, which is almost impossible, is a continued appreciation or healthy respect for the street and for the wild earth. Because when you look at the world from here, it's like what a friend of mine calls: "Watching tennis played on a vertical court." In Washington people start talking about the "Middle East peace process," and about how Shamir is going to accept this plan and Arafat that plan. And all I can do is sit back and say to myself, "Yes, but what about my grocer in Jerusalem? What will he accept?" What about the wild earth? The first thing that happens to you when you come to Washington is you lose touch with that wild earth. And when you lose touch with the wild earth you are always going to be surprised by something, whether you are an official or a journalist or an author.

Washington, D.C., 1990

THOMAS L. FRIEDMAN was a correspondent for UPI before joining *The New York Times* as a financial reporter. Among the many posts he has held at the *Times* are those of chief diplomatic correspondent, chief White House correspondent, and currently Foreign Affairs columnist. Mr. Friedman received two Pulitzer Prizes for his Mideast coverage, and the National Book Award in 1989 for *From Beirut to Jerusalem*.

Interview

J. Anthony Lukas

Did you always want to be a writer?

No. Initially, I dreamed of becoming an actor. My mother was an actress. She used to direct my brother and me in playlets —which I ultimately began to write—on the window seats of our house in White Plains. But my most important theatrical influence was my second cousin Paul Lukas—we called him Uncle Paul—who had won the Academy Award and had been to the White House to perform in his great hit, *Watch on the Rhine,* for the Roosevelts. He was a compelling figure; I hankered to follow in his footsteps.

In the summer after my junior year in high school I went to the Bass Rock Summer Theater, near Gloucester, Massachusetts, as assistant stage manager. The theater got into bad financial shape in midsummer and began casting young interns like me in significant roles. I drew a part in one of the worst clinkers in the entire theatrical repertory, a play called *Pappa Is All.* After opening night, *The Gloucester Times* said, "Young Mr. Lukas took the audience by storm last night. He has a great future in the American theater." I called my father, a New York lawyer, and read him the review. He feigned enthusiasm: he had a thing for actresses (he married two of them), but he did not want his son on the stage. So he called Uncle Paul in Hollywood and said, in effect, "You got us into this, you get us out of this."

Paul flew up to Gloucester to see the show. For that occasion, I put on my most bravura performance. Afterward, he took me down to a lobster restaurant on the Gloucester waterfront. Here I was, seventeen years old, having dinner with my idol, the Academy Award winner, fresh from my own theatrical "triumph," and still with my makeup on because I hoped that some women at adjoining tables would say, "My, who is that handsome young actor with Paul Lukas?" Paul bought me my first dry martini ever. Then, leaning across the table, he said in his deep Hungarian matinee-idol's voice, "Tony, you ver vonderful, vonderful,"–dramatic pause–"but not good enough." He went on to explain to me that I might find some decent roles now and then, but I'd never be a star–like him. I gave up the theater that night.

Within months I'd switched careers–I was extremely purposeful, much too purposeful, I think now–and plunged immediately into journalism. If I couldn't be center stage, I thought, then why not take a seat in the fourth row on the aisle, why not be a reporter of the great theater of events? Indeed, it has occurred to me of late that most of the subjects I've chosen to concentrate on–in long magazine pieces or books, at least–are highly theatrical. That's not bad, I suppose, because theatrical events, by definition, lend themselves to compelling retelling. It is bad, I suppose because a great many important stories in our society are not naturally theatrical. I'm a firm believer that journalism needs people to write searchingly about such subjects, but I can't be one of them. Although –come to think of it–I imagine many people would have said in 1976 that school desegregation in Boston was not an inherently theatrical subject. That brings us to *Common Ground.* I confess I enjoyed the challenge of writing a compelling, indeed a theatrical, book on a subject that some people frankly found tedious.

What then brought you to its subject matter?

My last book before *Common Ground* dealt with another theatrical subject–Watergate. But after I finished I realized that I'd been looking at it from long distance: I wanted to get closer to my next subject. Yet I didn't know what I wanted to write about. Most writers, I think, want to write the kind of books they like to read. So, not having read about anything much except Richard Nixon for a couple of years–what a depressing thought!–I went down to a bookstore on Fifth Avenue and picked out seven brand-new hardcover books that looked compelling. The second book I read was *Friendly Fire* and I was so taken by the way C. D. B. Bryan seemed to be at the breakfast table with the Iowa farm family that he wrote about, I decided then and there that I wanted to do a book with a family–or several families–at the center of it.

The precise arena came a few months later, when I read a news story about an angry crowd that drove Teddy Kennedy off a speaker's stand in Boston and into the federal building that bore his brother's name, just as school desegregation was beginning there. I remember asking myself, "What in the world is going on when Ted Kennedy is driven to take shelter by his 'own people,' Boston's Irish Catholics?" When a reporter asks himself "What in the world is going on?" that's generally a pretty good starting place for a story–or a book. In fact, absent that kind of obsessive curiosity, I can't produce a successful book.

Had you thought of writing about families, your own or others, before this?

All writers, I think, are, to one extent or another, damaged people. Writing is our way of repairing ourselves. In my own case, I was filing a hole in my life that opened at the age of eight, when my mother killed herself, throwing our family into utter disarray. My father quickly developed tuberculosis—psychosomatically triggered, the doctors thought—forcing him to seek treatment in an Arizona sanatorium. We sold our house, and my brother and I were shipped off to boarding school. Effectively, from the age of eight, I had no family, and certainly no community. That's one reason the book worked: I wasn't just writing a book about busing. I was filling a hole in myself.

How did you find the three different families you write about in *Common Ground*?

The first of the three families I found in Charlestown, the site of the Battle of Bunker Hill. I decided to set some of the book there when I went one day to the top of Bunker Hill—it's actually Breed's Hill, the soldiers got confused—and stood looking down at the wharves that ring the peninsula, and across the harbor to the golden dome of the State House. Above me towered the Bunker Hill Monument; in its shadow crouched Charlestown High School. Everywhere I looked I saw history. I wanted to capture that in my book. So I set out to find a Charlestown family that sent their kid to the high school and a black family that sent their kid to the same class.

To find the Irish family, I spent a whole evening drinking beer with Moe Gillen, a leader of the moderate wing of Charlestown's anti-busing movement. My hunch was that a lot of families I might go after would be reluctant to participate in the book without his imprimatur. He led me to one family and I worked with them for four years, until I finally concluded they wouldn't work in the book I wanted to write. They were fanatics, which was interesting, but the appropriate author for that book would have been not me, but Dostoevsky. Four years seems like a long time to waste—but it wasn't a waste. Through the first family I'd learned an awful lot about Charlestown. The family I ultimately chose—the McGoffs—were fish who swam in that same sea.

I found the black family, the Twymons, through a social worker in Boston's South End. They were the second black family he introduced me to. Rachel Twymon was so articulate and her children were so obviously eager to be in the book that I felt they'd be good to work with. Some members of Boston's black community didn't agree with my choice. They thought it was the "wrong family." One of Rachel's sons turned out to be a rapist. Two of her other sons had briefly turned their hand to mugging. But one uncle had a master's degree in social work; Rachel herself was chairwoman of the local community center. Troubled by that disjuncture, I consulted a black psychologist I knew in Cambridge and asked him if he thought I should drop the Twymons. He said: "Absolutely not. That kind of diversity is a very common pattern among blacks today, indeed among all ethnic groups as they come of age in America."

Finding those two families took some doing, but in many ways the most difficult choice was the third family: the white, middle-class family. I felt very strongly that the book needed a family from a different social class, who connected to school desegregation in a different way. Over a period of three months, I must have seen twenty-five such families, none of whom seemed quite right. Then a professor of law at Harvard sent me to see friends of his, the Divers. After an evening with them, I knew they were the family I'd been looking for.

Was it difficult gaining the confidence of your subjects?
That wasn't a tremendous feat. We all enjoy talking about ourselves to a sympathetic listener. I also struck an unusual agreement with the families. To get them to open up to me the way I hoped they would, I realized I couldn't ask them to live in total suspense about what I would do with their lives. So I let each family read the nine chapters about themselves, correct any matter of verifiable fact, and argue with me about matters of interpretation, so long as they understood that final interpretation was my responsibility. This agreement, by the way,

did not apply to public figures—the mayor, the judge, etc.—in *Common Ground.* They were people who had plenty of experience in dealing with the press, as the three families did not. This arrangement permitted us to catch about seventy small errors —a misspelling here, a wrong date there. None of the families ever charged me with betraying them. Indeed, I think all three of them were reasonably satisfied with the portrait I drew of them.

What was the greatest challenge for you in writing this book?
Organization. It was guided by three principles. First I wanted to braid the families' stories through one another, but without a mechanical rotation. Second, I wanted the book to move ahead chronologically: I wanted it to be a yarn—an instructive yarn, but a yarn nonetheless. Third—and this was the real killer —I wanted each of the thirty or so chapters to not only advance a family's story chronologically, but to address a different aspect of their lives.

Did you intentionally create suspense in the book? It reads like a mystery.
Yes, in the sense that I never wanted the reader to know whose drama I was most caught up in. We don't normally think of an author trying to sow confusion in his readers, but I did. I didn't want to lay out any lessons. Whatever lessons a reader might find in my book, I wanted them to seep out through the interstices of the three families.

There may not be any "truths"—as conventionally understood—in *Common Ground.* People often ask me how the experience of writing the book changed me, and I finally developed an answer that may seem flip, but it's what I felt. I said the book didn't take me from left to right or right to left, but from the party of simplicity to the party of complexity. If once I had read plain moral lessons in the school desegregation battle, I no longer found it so easy to say who was right and who was wrong. Moreover, I came to feel that none of these three families could be understood outside the context of a very complex past. Each individual in each family trailed behind him or her a long train of history: that individual's own history, their family history, and what I called their "tribal" history.

What was the best part for you about writing this book?

By the time I started the book, I was feeling increasingly dissatisfied with the heavily attributed style I had learned on the *Baltimore Sun* and *The New York Times.* I was experimenting with a narrative style in which, chapter by chapter, I saw these events through the eyes of each family. The secret of this technique was that I knew I always had the families themselves as a backstop. If I went too far afield–I called it "flying"–they'd bring me back to earth.

Ironically, four decades after that summer in Gloucester, I now find myself back in the theater, as *Common Ground* is being turned into a two-evening play at the Mark Taper Forum in Los Angeles, by the same people who developed *Angels in America.* I'm not writing it, but I'm working very closely with the playwright. If we succeed in getting this play staged in Los Angeles and ultimately in New York–it will be the ripening of an old and cherished dream.

New York, New York, 1994

J. ANTHONY LUKAS is the author of four books, including *Common Ground: A Turbulent Decade in the Lives of Three American Families,* which won the National Book Award for nonfiction as well as the Pulitzer Prize. He began his career as a journalist at the *Baltimore Sun,* and spent nine years at *The New York Times.*

The Reading Room, The New York Public Library

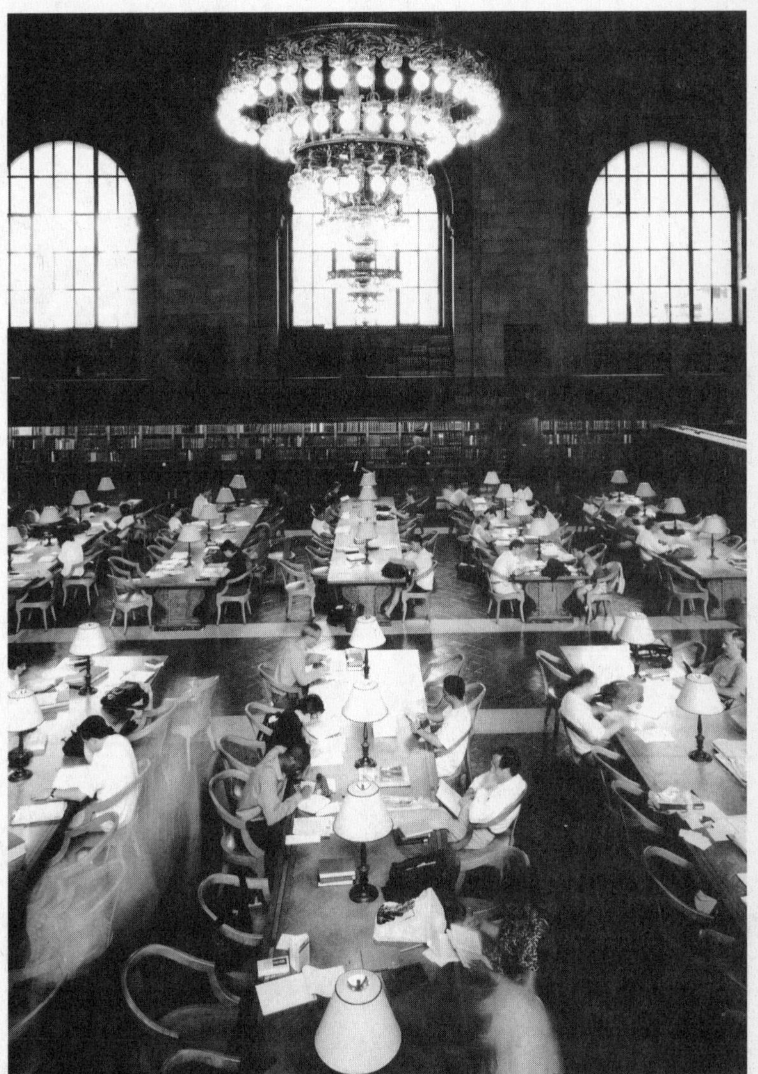

The Love of Books

Gloria Naylor

Any life amounts to "organized chaos": biologically we are more space than matter and that matter consists of careening atoms always in flux; psychologically we are minute electrical charges, running from the brain to the spinal cord, the organs, the hormonal systems. Sitting apart from that is a consciousness that orders, to our specific preferences, any given reality at any given time. A long way of saying: our lives are what we make them. And definitely our "writing lives," which is miming life in both its execution and its product. And so to make sense of the senseless, writers reach for metaphors to explain–to themselves and others–exactly what it is that they do. Those metaphors and the resultant explanations are value-laden; they spring from our specific culture and our personal politics.

Why do I write? The truth, the unvarnished truth, is that I haven't a clue. The answer to that question lies hidden in the same box that holds the origin of human creativity, our imperative need as a species to communicate, and to be touched. Many minds for many years have busied themselves trying to unlock that box, and writers, for the most part, are quite happy to allow the literary critics, anthropologists, psychologists, and biologists to argue interdiscipline and intradiscipline while they stay out of the fray. And when writers are invited in, they'll reach for some shorthand, some metaphor, to throw quickly into the ring so they can get back to doing—for whatever reason—what they do best.

I normally reach for a poem called "The Unclaimed," by Nikky Finney, a young African-American woman who evokes the spirit of all the women in her past "whose names do not ripple in neon lights or whose distinctiveness has yet to be embedded on printed paper." These women, the poet tells us, were never allowed time to pamper themselves in front of mirrors or even time to cry. They were women who sang over stovetops and wash-tubs; scribbled poems on bits of paper and dinner napkins—women who acted out the drama of their lives unsung and forgotten. And so she concludes:

for all that you were
for all that you always wanted to be
each time i sign my name
know that it is for a thousand like you
who could not hold a pen
but who instead held me
and rocked me gently
to the creative rhythms
i now live by

I elect to trace the untraceable, my passionate love of books and my affair with the written word, back to my mother, who was also an avid lover of books. She and my father were from sharecropping families and grew up in the 1930s in Mississippi. She was not allowed to use the public libraries; and purchasing books was out of the question for her. What many young people tend to forget today, in the age of excessiveness and of almost ingrained waste that we have in consumerist America, is that books were once a luxury for people until the advent of the ten-cent novel which ultimately evolved into the paperback.

Most people, especially working-class and poor people, were not able to buy books so they depended on the public libraries. That was why Ben Franklin instituted the free lending library, hoping to give the children of the working class at least a competitive edge with the children of the upper classes, who could afford to have books.

My mother was one of eight children and her family worked collectively on a farm from Monday to Friday to bring in the requisite crop–for them it was cotton. Since this was in the South, in the Bible Belt, it meant that Sunday was spent in church–all day. Saturday was then the only free time my mother had. So while her sisters and brothers went off to town to spend their time, she would hire herself out in someone else's field on her free Saturdays. For that labor, she received fifty cents–a day but it was her fifty cents. At the end of the month she had two dollars and she would take that two dollars and send away to book clubs. And that's how she got her reading material.

She made a vow to herself that she would never raise a child in the South. It is ironic that when my parents, in 1949, moved north to New York City, they left behind a region that would eventually become a place much more conducive for African-Americans to hold power than the place to which they fled. But who was to know the future? My mother only knew her past. And her history spoke loud and clear: if you were poor, and if you were black in Tunica County, you were not going to read. She always told my sisters and me that she was not ashamed of her background–it was no sin to be poor. But the greatest sin is to keep people from learning to dream. And my mother believed that books taught the young how to dream. She knew. of course, that she would not be eradicating racism from her life by moving, as Malcolm X said, "from down South to up South." But she was aware that, in New York City at least, her tax dollars would go to support public institutions that would be open to her children.

Because we grew up without much money and a whole lot of dreams, we spent a great deal of time in the public libraries.

The law in New York was that a child had to be able to write their name in order to get a juvenile library card. But before my sisters and I had even attained the age of literacy, my mother would take us on these pilgrimages to the library. They live in my mind as small dark rooms with heavy wood bookcases and the heavy desks of the librarian, who looked like Olive Oyl. My mother would say, "Do you see all these books? Once you can write your name, all of these books will be yours. For two weeks. But yours."

I had to get much older to understand why she took us on those pilgrimages. While indeed it was to educate us, I think it was also to heal some place within herself. For me it made the library a place that was quite familiar, a place that was even welcoming. I was eager to be able to qualify to enter those doors. I was eager to discover whatever mystery was within the ink upon that paper, because also within me–and this had to be genetic–was a fascination with the written word. I used to love the feel and the heft of a book. In those days, they were made with a certain kind of glue and when you broke the binding you could smell that special glue. I'm not saying I was getting high off that glue. There was just this wonderful, earthy smell to it.

My mother didn't know then and, of course, at four and five I didn't know that I was on my way to being a very shy and very repressed adolescent. Books were to be my only avenue out of the walls my emotions built around me in those years. I felt trapped within my home and trapped within school, and it was through the pages of books that I was released into other worlds. I literally read my way from the A's to the Z's in the children's section of the library. I can still see that two-shelf row of books, and it ran the whole length of the room. Louisa May Alcott's, I recall, was the first set of books–*Little Women,* and *Little Men,* and *Jo's Boys,* and *Under the Umbrella*–she wrote a whole slew of books following those young women from adolescence into adulthood. I can remember reading all the way through to the last author because there was another set of books by Laura Ingalls Wilder–*Little House on the Prairie, Little House in the Big*

Woods, Those Happy Golden Years. Once again following a young girl in her coming-of-age from adolescence all the way into adulthood and marriage. It was the world through which I lived.

I don't believe this would have been enough to have created a writer, although most writers first begin as avid readers. But a writer needs something else–a conscious connection between the validity of their personal experiences and the page. My shyness kept me from communicating verbally, to the point that my teachers thought perhaps I was slow. The theory of education in those years–the fifties and early sixties–held that a well-rounded child participated in class. That meant raising your hand, which for a child like me meant to break out in a cold sweat. The idea that I had to step forth and give voice to something was a nightmare.

My mother, seeing that I was not a talker and understanding that indeed I was, of the three girls, perhaps her most gifted child (the teachers came to understand that later as well because I always excelled in the written tests) went out to Woolworth's and bought me one of those white plastic diaries. I think they went for something like ninety-nine cents in those days, and stamped on it in gold leaf was "One Year Diary"–the kind with the cheap lock your sister could open with a bobby pin. My mother said, "You know, Gloria, I'll bet there are a lot of things going on in the world you don't understand and I'm sure there are even things going on in here in our home that might be troubling you, but since you can't seem to talk to your father and me about these things, why don't you write them down in here." She threw the book on the bed and was wise enough to leave the room, and not belabor the point. I picked up the diary and I did just that, I proceeded to write down all the things that I could not say.

From the age of twelve I made the vital connection between inarticulate feeling and the written word. Whatever went into those original pages are not eternal keepsakes, they are not classic thoughts, but they were my feelings, it was my pain, and the pain was real to me at twelve years old. And we wonder about the rise in teenage suicides. It is because adults resist believing that whatever the demons are, if they're twelve-year-old, thirteen-year-old, fourteen-year-old demons, they are *real.* I know; I had them.

Through the luck of the draw of having a very wise and perceptive mother who happened to match what I needed with the gift of that diary, my life was saved. Because those feelings were going to come out. I was going to speak one day. But the horrifying question is, In what language would those feelings have been expressed? I paraphrase Toni Morrison in *Sula*: An artist without an art form is a dangerous thing. It is probably one of the most dangerous things on this earth. And being a female in the 1960s, I would have, I think, directed that destruction inward as opposed to outward. But instead, I filled up that diary, and then proceeded to fill up the spare pages in my loose-leaf notebook at the end of the school year with my ramblings that slowly turned into poems. The poems slowly evolved into *Twilight Zone*-type short stories—I have always been enamored somehow with the mystical and the idea of alternative realities, and began writing supernatural stories even as an adolescent.

But it took until I was twenty-seven years old for me to believe that I had the faintest chance of being a writer. I went through my adolescence and young adulthood being told that black people did not write books. How did this come about? I was a kid who read to the tune of a book a day, who had been "discovered" by her middle-school teachers, who plied me with extra reading, which I would take home on the weekends. In those hundreds of texts that I read, there was nothing about black Americans or by black Americans. Those authors weren't on the shelves in the public libraries in New York City, and they definitely weren't on my standard junior high school or high school curriculum. If black people had written books, would I not have read them? Would I not have been taught them? If Gwendolyn Brooks had indeed won the Pulitzer Prize the year she did, 1950 (ironically the year I was born), should she not qualify as a talented enough American writer to be on my syllabus?

We do not have to say to our children, "You are nothing."

We don't have to stand up in an auditorium, on a parade ground, and blatantly shout out to them, "You are have nothing to give." We have done this much more effectively, through silence, through what they do *not* see, through what is *not* there when we parade before them what we declare is worthy. It is a very effective message. It was the one that I received. And I received it from well-meaning people, who thought I was bright, I had a future, I had promise. I took the unrest in the sixties and the kids then in their late teens and early twenties, who were willing to put their careers on the line, their lives on the line–and some lost them at Jackson and Kent State–in order to give birth to the educational institutions that began to exist in the mid seventies. Ones which taught what America really was, that provided an education that edified and represented the entire citizenry. This was the gift that they gave me. And so by the time I entered Brooklyn College, once again an institution supported by public funds, there was an Africana Studies Department, a Women's Studies Program, Chicano Studies (as they were called in those years), Asian Studies. And I then was able to encounter the works of Ralph Ellison, Toni Morrison, Nikki Giovanni, James Baldwin, Richard Wright, Zora Neale Hurston...the list goes on and on. We're not talking about people who deserved a Black Literature Day or a Black Literature Hour in our curriculums. These are names that will be here in the year 3000, because they have helped to define not only American literature, but world literature. I owe those young people who spilled their blood in the sixties a huge debt of gratitude, because by learning that there was this heritage of writers behind me, and specifically black female writers, when I looked in the mirror there was the image I desperately needed to see. What I had seen previously was no image. Slowly, by completing my diet with these books, an outline was filled in. And that outline did not say that black was beautiful, it did not say that black was ugly. It said simply: you are. You exist. It reverberated enough to give me the courage to pick up the pen. And it's what finally validated me.

My first novel, *The Women of Brewster Place,* literally began that very semester at Brooklyn College when I discovered that there was a whole history of black writing in America; and that I had foremothers and forefathers who stood behind me with the ghosts of their excellence. And I was determined that if I had only one novel in me, I was going to write about what I had not had, in those twenty-some odd years of literacy, the privilege to read about. I was going to write all about me. And I knew that if I just chose one female character, one protagonist, she could not do justice to the diversity of the black female experience in America. One woman couldn't do it all. So I hit upon the structure of having different chapters devoted to the lives of different women. I can remember making a mental list of how they would differ. They were to vary, beginning with something as superficial as their skin colors. I know it's not currently in vogue but I do like the word "colored." Because when I look around, that's what I see–colored people–pink on up in the European American; then moving from alabaster to ebony in the black female. We also range from being devotedly religious to almost irreligious. We are young and old. We are political, nonpolitical. We even differ in our sexual preferences. So on this dead-end street, I had hoped to create a whole panorama of what it meant to be black and female in America. To claim and to validate as many lives as I possibly could. To give them each the dignity that I felt they each deserved. To this day I still call that book–which is now fifteen years old–my love letter to the black woman in America. But it first began as a love letter to myself. And by beginning with what was indeed a very visceral and personal statement it had reverberated and touched women all over the world. I have received letters from as far away as Japan, from Korean women who inform me that they are a minority within that society. They saw their own grandparents and aunts on that dead-end street.

Every writer must articulate from the specific. They must reach down where they stand, because there is nothing else from which to draw. Therefore were I to go along with the traditional view that the Western literature began with Homer (a good argument to the contrary is the subject of another essay)—Homer didn't write about the Romans, nor the Phoenicians, nor about the Huns. He wrote about the Greeks because that's what he was. Shakespeare wrote about Elizabethan Englishmen. He put them in the Caribbean, he put them in Denmark, he put them in Verona—but they were all Elizabethan Englishmen. Joyce wrote about the Irish; Philip Roth writes about the Jews, Maxine Hong Kingston about Chinese-Americans. You write where you are. It's the only thing you have to give. And if you are fortunate enough, there is a spark that will somehow ignite a work so that it touches almost anyone who reads it, although it is about a very specific people at a very specific time. And so that's what I attempt to do with my work—to reach down where I am and to articulate those lives. I could spend my entire life, what I have left of a natural life span, writing only about the Brewster Places in America and never exhaust that which is universal to it.

What I plan to do though with the rest of my life is indeed to communicate with images. They will not always be written images. I love working for the stage. I will write for film. I will always have stories to tell. They may not be good stories, they may not be bad stories. But I would like to believe that I will always tell honest stories and that to the lives that come to me I will somehow do them justice.

Columbia, Maryland, 1995

GLORIA NAYLOR is the author of four novels, among them *The Women of Brewster Place,* which won a National Book Award and was made into a television mini-series.Her novel *Bailey's Café* was adapted for the stage. The recipient of numerous academic honors, Ms. Naylor is the president of One Way Productions, which develops programming for stage and screen.

Stubborn Facts and Fickle Realities: Research for Nonfiction

Ron Chernow

While collecting my thoughts about nonfiction writing, I stumbled upon the title "Stubborn Facts and Fickle Realities." Once it popped into my head, I fell hopelessly in love with it. I had no idea what it meant, but couldn't quite dislodge it from my mind. I was like a happily married man, suddenly in the thrall of a beautiful, tyrannical mistress. Luckily, I realized that my subconscious mind had considerately supplied me with an opening wedge into my subject—the nature of nonfiction writing, specifically, historical writing, and even more specifically, financial historical writing. I must sound a bit like Polonius.

The House of Morgan, I should explain, was my first book and something of a fairytale experience. It received fine reviews (except for a couple of well-placed stinkers), then won the National Book Award. Winning the National Book Award for your first book, by the way, is an efficient way to lose your writer friends. People are cheered by your success—but only up to a point.

Before embarking on the book, I had my only grown-up job, a nine-to-five stint at an impressive-sounding place called the Twentieth Century Fund, a public policy foundation where I bore the fancy title of Program Officer. The fancy title was meant to compensate for the very *un*fancy salary. Having been a freelance business writer for many years, I was now placed in charge of books on the changing financial scene. This not only gave me a crash course in economics, but provided me with a front-row seat to watch the merger mania and wild bull market sweeping Wall Street. At the same time I was studying all the previous merger fads and bull markets in financial history.

By late 1986, it should have been clear to the most humble panhandler and financial illiterate on Main Street that a stock-market crash of major proportions was imminent. Our major newspapers were printing graphs of the Dow Jones averages of the 1920s superimposed on those of the 1980s, showing the parallel peaks and troughs. This eerie resemblance, clearly, was more than coincidental. As Red Buttons used to sing, "Strange things were happening." I remember everybody in my office saying, "Oh, my God. This is like 1929. There's going to be a stock-market crash." The only person who dissented was a rich young man fully invested in common stocks. Each morning, he would surface from the depths of the stock-market listings with a glassy-eyed smile that left the rest of us feeling slightly envious and resentful. Not surprisingly, the one person who didn't see that the party would soon fizzle was the only one who had been invited in the first place.

I had a tiny intuition—a mini-flicker of a brainstorm—that the market would collapse, the merger vogue would abruptly end, credit would crunch, banks would topple, real estate prices would nosedive, and the public would rise up in populist rage. How was I endowed with such prophetic intelligence? Quite simply, I had studied the previous boom-and-bust cycles and they followed certain enduring patterns. During periods of easy credit, real estate prices soared in tandem with stocks. When credit contracted, they plunged together. Do you know the tale of the Empire State Building? It was conceived in 1928 by John Jacob Raskob as a monument to Wall Street glory. By the time it was completed in 1931, the market sagged under such a glut of office space that cruel wags christened it the Empty State Building. Remember that lilting Gershwin tune—"They all laughed at Rockefeller Center, now they're fighting to get in"? They were laughing at Rockefeller Center because after the 1929 crash, with a five-to-ten year surplus of office space, it was considered pure folly to construct a large urban complex during the Depression, as the Rockefeller family did.

So I figured that when the day of financial Armageddon arrived, the public—battered, disillusioned, and terribly cranky—might be ripe for a hefty saga of Wall Street. They would want to know why this debacle of busted banks and real estate deflation had occurred. I cast about for the story of a family or firm that would serve as a vehicle for the story of American high finance. This led me straight to that mysterious marble building at 23 Wall Street called the House of Morgan. Through 150 years of almost monotonous success, the Morgans had stood at the pinnacle of Wall Street, and through the prism of their story I hoped to glimpse the entire, crazy panorama of American finance. If the concept ultimately worked, the Morgans deserved the credit. To stay atop the world of investment banking is a slippery trick for even a decade—as junk-bond king Michael Milken discovered. To hug the top of that well-greased pole for over a century—well, that's extraordinary, and only the Rothschilds, the Warburgs, and a few other banking families have managed that feat.

Before setting out on my Morgan adventure, I was, as far as I can tell, a normal person. Before 1987, nobody considered me a strange bird. I didn't yet wear a dog tag that stamped me as "Ron Chernow, The Banking Historian." However, during the two and a half years that I labored on my massive tome, I started to get queer looks from people at parties—subtle, but unmistakable hints. When I told them I was writing a long banking history and expected it to sell, they looked at me quizzically, as if wondering, "Is he putting me on?" Or else they gave me tender, pitying stares, as if I were a young man gripped by a severe delusion that would be cured by time. Perhaps they expected to find me someday stumbling around the grounds of a sanatorium, picking papers off the grass.

At times, I, too, wondered whether I had given way to masochism or a bizarre disease. A passionate interest in banking didn't seem healthy so much as strange and unnatural. Yeats wrote about "the fascination of what's difficult." Maybe that accounted for my attraction to finance. I'm equally reminded of Conrad's phrase about "the fascination of the abomination," which is perhaps closer to the mark.

The House of Morgan proved a huge success. Against all odds, it made several regional bestseller lists and won awards. Perhaps I was helped by my uncomfortable encounters with those skeptical partygoers. Because of their incredulity I didn't assume that my readers would be kindly or tolerant souls. Rather, I pictured them as humorless sadists with short attention spans, who would keep glancing at their watches, demanding to know how I expected them to read a long book about banking. So I had to work the whole bag of writer tricks: I crooned, hoofed, juggled, swallowed fire, balanced boxes, spun saucers, did cartwheels–anything to keep the restive crowd under the Big Top.

While researching my book, I must have read, in whole or part, two hundred books on financial history, most of them written in deadly, leaden prose. My eyes acquired the hooded squint of people who have endured months of trench warfare. These books convinced me that financial history is the bastard child of the profession. There were some fine, even brilliant things, but mostly dusty heaps of incurable pedantry. As I wandered about those mildewed shelves in the least used corner of the library, I realized that it wouldn't be hard to make a name in this dreary wasteland. Even an anthill would stand out as a majestic, snow-capped Everest in the flat landscape of financial history.

As I spent more time there, this section of the library did turn out to have some compensatory charm. I began to notice a pattern. Bull markets on Wall Street had, typically, produced bull markets in books *about* Wall Street. And the writers, I must say, fared far better than the bankers, because when boom finally curdled into bust and bankers took fancy swan dives from upper-story ledges, the writers cashed in on their *second* bull market, swooping down to describe the financial wreckage. In boom times, you get books of glorification; during bust, of disenchantment. After having been hailed as heroic figures in the 1920s, bankers were called banksters–to rhyme with gangsters–in the 1930s.

Financial writing has, in fact, had a long and distinguished history in America. It just comes in sudden spurts. Unlike mainstream history, financial history goes through long moribund stretches followed by brief periods of hectic activity. Every generation or so, financial markets swell up on a tidal wave of cash and credit that permits all manner of mayhem and speculation. These compressed periods of frenzy tend to attract some very colorful writers, such as Frederick Lewis Allen, who wrote *The Great Pierpont Morgan,* the best brief account of the tycoon.

During the past decade, we've been on such a financial roller-coaster that we forget Wall Street can be a sleepy locale. In the 1930s, things grew so sluggish at the New York Stock Exchange that bored traders invented games to pass the time. During the Depression, stockbrokers took days off to ply the more lucrative apple trade on street corners–these vacations were called Apple Days. In the 1950s and early 1960s, Wall Street was a place of terminal ennui and, with few exceptions, attracted powerfully dull writers. It even took time for the extreme theatrics of the 1980s to generate good books. When I began *The House of Morgan* in late 1986, there was scarcely a whisper of protest abroad about the Wall Street antics. The Yuppie dealmakers, festooned in red suspenders with beepers on their belts, were undisputed darlings of the business press, as they allegedly reshaped the American economy through hostile raids and leveraged buyouts. I foresaw my book as a corrective to the prevailing euphoria.

By the time the book appeared in March 1990, the pendulum had veered so violently to the other extreme that two reviewers even chided me for being too soft on bankers. Clearly a disabused public was in an ugly, lynch-mob mood, and writers, to succeed, had to flay the bloody bankers red and raw. This new mood was mirrored in a whole slew of books. Michael Lewis had just published *Liar's Poker,* his witty glimpse of Salomon Brothers in which the training program for young bond traders makes Marine boot camp look like sissy stuff. Then Bryan Burrough and John Helyar wrote *Barbarians at the Gate* about the unseemly scramble to take over RJR Nabisco. There are moments in that Grand Guignol when Peter Cohen, head of Shearson Lehman American Express, sounds as if he's doing a crude imitation of Edward G. Robinson in *Little Caesar.* There was also *Den of Thieves* by James Stewart, in which the banksters sound more like gangsters, plain and simple. Some of this moralistic rage reflected the national embarrassment that we had so recently idealized these same people. What better way to purge guilt than through an orgy of self-righteous indignation?

As much as I admire these books—and I genuinely do, they're all well-written and gripping stories and virtuoso reporting jobs—I don't find them loaded with stubborn facts or fickle realities. I find lots of tame facts that do the writers' bidding to create unambiguous, one-dimensional realities. They're painted in the bold, bright colors of pop journalism, not in the more muted, delicate shades of history.

There are two ways, I think, to approach nonfiction writing. You can set out on your journey armed with a thesis and collect supporting facts along the way—a perfectly legitimate approach. From this prosecutorial style, we get our best polemics, satires, and exposés. Partisan, one-sided, and tending to justify a preconceived viewpoint, this is the art of the legal brief and indictment. This literature more often sounds like a trumpet blast, a call to arms, than an invitation to sober analysis and reflection.

But there's another type of nonfiction writing in which the writer surrenders all preconceived belief and submits to the material. That's not to say that the latter writers are mental eunuchs without firm opinions or airheads mindlessly soaking up facts. They, too, begin their journey freighted with the bulky baggage of prejudice, although they may not know it or admit to it. The difference is that they zealously search for facts that contradict their working hypotheses. They like to stub their toes on hard, uncomfortable facts strewn in their paths. They want information that will explode, like a prankster's cigar, in their faces.

I prefer to fancy that I'm a member of this second group. I'm intrigued by realities that are buried deep, and are tough to ferret out. This complex, ambiguous reality is usually far more fascinating than the stereotypical notions we start out with. The pursuit of such truth can be long and exhausting, but highly stimulating. Instead of speeding down some big boring Interstate of research, paved by many previous writers, one takes a detour through strange, forbidding landscapes. Janet Leigh would never have met Anthony Perkins at the Bates Motel had she not turned off the highway. This is true in historical research as well. If you want to meet the true originals, turn off the main highway. Yes, take a walk on the wild side.

In writing about the Morgans, I didn't deliberately set out to dash stereotypes or write a revisionist history. Actually I was amazed when some reviewers called it a revisionist book, because I didn't know I had perpetrated any such creature. On the other hand, I knew that I had been on the qui vive for stubborn facts and fickle realities. Take the case of J. Pierpont Morgan, who died in 1913. In a celebrated Steichen photo, he stares out at the viewer with a fierce glare and grotesquely bulbous nose. It seems as if he wants to strangle the photographer –which was precisely the case. To accentuate Morgan's nose, Steichen wanted him to pose in profile. Morgan, no dope, gazed straight ahead. Finally, he began to rise up out of his seat to strangle the young photographer. At that moment, Steichen snapped the unforgettable image.

J. Pierpont Morgan was said to be the most powerful citizen on Planet Earth, and he was no shrinking violet. He controlled one-third of American railroads at a time when railroad stocks comprised 60 percent of the stocks on the New York Stock Exchange. After he created U.S. Steel in 1901–the first billion-dollar corporation–he controlled 70 percent of the steel industry. He ruled much of the North Atlantic shipping. And just in case he had a few moments to spare at day's end, he also dominated the three largest insurance companies. Beside his Morgan bank, he controlled Guaranty Trust, Bankers Trust, and held sizable stakes in what became Chase Manhattan and Citicorp.

Once Morgan offhandedly remarked, "America is good enough for me," and the *Commoner,* the newspaper of William Jennings Bryan, shot back, "Whenever you don't like it, you can give it back." Morgan lived in unutterably regal splendor. His yacht measured over 300 feet at the waterline–twenty feet longer than the monstrosity later owned by Donald Trump– and required a crew of seventy. According to legend, when this dreadnought appeared in foreign ports, the natives panicked, fearing the start of an American financial invasion. At one point, when Morgan was trying to take over the North Atlantic shipping industry *and* the London underground system, vendors on London sidewalks hawked satirical penny sheets entitled, "License to Stay on the Planet Earth," signed with a flourish at the bottom, "J. Pierpont Morgan."

Morgan has often been presented as an ogre, a robber baron, a public-be-damned tyrant who scorned the people's representatives. There was truth to this image, but it wasn't the whole truth. As a young man, Pierpont had wed a fragile, sensitive young woman named Mimi who had tuberculosis when he married her. He had to prop her up during the wedding ceremony and carry her to a waiting carriage. It indeed sounds like a saccharin Victorian novel. During their four-month honeymoon, Pierpont took her around the Mediterranean, trying to find a doctor who could cure her. She died on the honeymoon and he mourned her for the rest of his life, making annual pilgrimages to her grave.

This isn't exactly the caddish, brutish behavior associated with card-carrying robber barons. In fact, the more I learned about Morgan, the more I found a surprisingly lonely, vulnerable character hiding behind the fire-breathing facade. To me, this was a far more interesting portrait than the familiar caricature and it acquired extra force by the constant, tacit contrast with the historical cartoon.

As to serious political and financial issues raised by Morgan's story, I tried to ask new questions rather than to assume an open-and-shut case, with the populists always right and the tycoons, by definition, wrong. For instance, it was well-known that Morgan had autocratically ruled many companies he had financed. He sat on their boards and if anybody dared to dispute him, he would fling his matchbox against the wall, slam his fist on the table, and bellow, "Gentlemen, let's take a vote. Let's see where these gentlemen stand." By that point, the gentlemen were cowering and acceded to his wishes.

I wanted to find out why companies allowed themselves to be so enslaved. While reformers clamored to liberate these poor folks from the evil Morgan bank, the companies themselves didn't seem in any particular hurry to shake off their golden chains, and cherished their servitude. Why? At that stage in industrial development, the Morgan bank was often better known than its clients, so that Morgan patronage won them credit on better terms than they could acquire on their own.

It was a badge of pride that they had been accepted as exclusive Morgan clients.

If I asked new questions about the Morgans, it was as much from concern for the present as the past. If you stare at any historical work long enough, you will discern the pale, ghostly reflection of the author and his period. I was scribbling my book amid merger mania on Wall Street and universal condemnation of its short-term profit orientation. Raiders were buying companies, dismantling them to make a killing, then walking away. So when I read the earlier reformers' tirades against the Morgans for being involved with companies for decades on end, I had a different reaction from that of such reformers as Louis Brandeis. The old tycoons had been faulted precisely for their *long-term* involvement with clients. Generations of Morgans sat on the boards of U.S. Steel, AT&T, and General Motors. Problems of conflict-of-interest and excessive concentration of power abounded, but I'm not sure the American economy suffered as a result.

Perhaps because Morgan had been painted in such ghastly colors, I was struck by his redeeming features. But I'm no less skeptical when presented with those winged saints who populate many official histories and authorized biographies in the business world. I had a case of this sort with the senior Morgan partner of the Jazz Age and Depression, Thomas W. Lamont, a smoothly elegant character who hosted glamorous black-tie dinners at his Manhattan townhouse. He befriended numerous celebrities, including Walter Lippmann, John Galsworthy, and H. G. Wells. Because he handled Morgan relations with foreign governments, Lamont carried the nickname of Secretary of State of the Morgan empire. He was, arguably, the world's most influential financier between the two world wars.

I was astonished that nobody had written a biography of Thomas W. Lamont. In a world ravenous for biographical subjects, this omission was baffling. When I read Lamont's 1948 obituary in *The New York Times,* I discovered the reason.

The obituary wasn't on the bottom of the front page but on the *top,* as if a head of state had died, and the article that followed portrayed a flawless human being. It was patent why nobody had written about Lamont—he not only sounded too good to be true, but too good to be interesting. All that most people knew about him was that he had presided over the bankers' rescue on Black Thursday, 1929. When reporters surged around him that day to elicit his reaction to the crash, he uttered the classic understatement in American financial history: "There has been a little distress selling."

Nobody had rummaged through Lamont's voluminous papers at Harvard, which offer a vivid, comprehensive portrait of Morgan dealings between the world wars with presidents, prime ministers, and even the Vatican. During my first day's work at Harvard, I read his unpublished correspondence with Brandeis, Franklin Roosevelt, Nancy Astor, Henry Ford, and Walter Lippmann. That night, I telephoned my wife and said, "I've hit the Comstock Lode."

Was Lamont the plaster saint of *The New York Times* obituary? Of course not. Choirboys don't ascend to the top of Wall Street investment houses. It turned out that he was no shining liberal, but the personal banker to Benito Mussolini. His attentive service to *Il Duce* went far beyond the merely financial. On behalf of Mussolini, Lamont lobbied his close friend Walter Lippmann, a vocal critic of *Il Duce,* and set up a secret publicity bureau to burnish the dictator's image in the U.S. He even fed public relations tips to Mussolini, some of them extremely distasteful. After Mussolini invaded Ethiopia in 1935, Lamont suggested that to sway Anglo-Saxon opinion he liken this bloody conquest to the settling of the American West. I found many ironies about Lamont's life, including the wonderful memo he sent to Herbert Hoover five days before Black Thursday, telling him not to worry about the dizzying gyrations on Wall Street. The memo ended with the immortal words, "The future appears brilliant."

Even if a historian takes the dangerous detour and checks into the sinister Bates Motel, he or she must frame the stubborn facts into a narrative. History, obviously, is more than just gathering sweepings from the world's libraries. One must end up with a vision that will make the narrative sing and recreate the period. To do this, one must marinate the stubborn facts in the rich broth of the imagination over an extended period.

This process is not as different from writing fiction as you might think. No less than the novelist, the historian carries his cast of characters around in his head. To express them, he must internalize them, getting to know them as intimately as actors know the characters they play. This imaginative interplay between author and subject brings the personalities to life, giving them the roundness and cohesion of figures in a novel. To accomplish this, you need far more than just an interesting set of facts. You need that special intuition that glues facts together in a true, absorbing, and revealing way.

Strange things happen as we brood about historical figures. While writing the Morgan book, I became obsessed by Thomas W. Lamont. His ghost attended me everywhere. At first, I was perplexed by this, for we were outwardly so different. Then I realized that if *I* had been a banker in the Jazz Age, I would have tried to be a Thomas W. Lamont. This urbane, polished man was an ex-newspaper reporter and a badly frustrated writer who constantly tried to transcend the narrow confines of banking. While making loans to Italy, he worked at a beautiful Italian refectory table or hosted meetings of the Dante Society at his home or took picnics in the Roman countryside. He tried to convert banking into an intensely personal, cultural experience. Without quite realizing it, I had been vicariously living his life, trying it on for size. That's probably why his portrait was, to my mind, the most compelling in my book.

So the writing of history starts by colliding with stubborn facts, but then the imagination weaves a bit of fancy around those facts. As in fiction, you develop complicated relationships with your characters. You love them, hate them, fight with them, make up. That's why, in the end, the book is as much about the author as his subject. The Morgans are on every page of *The House of Morgan,* but for better or worse, so am I. As the writer strolls, unsuspecting, down the corridor of history, it often turns into a nightmarish hall of mirrors in which he keeps catching distorted glimpses of himself.

Fidelity to facts is not a license to be a bore or evade hard questions or fudge tough issues. It doesn't mean providing the reader with a dry meal of sawdust. Rather, it suggests a richer, more challenging route for arriving at visions–those visions that future generations of historians will inevitably deride as the stale cartoons and sterile myths of yesteryear.

Chicago, Illinois, 1992

RON CHERNOW is the author of *The House of Morgan,* which won the National Book Award for nonfiction, and *The Warburgs.* A longtime magazine writer, radio commentator, and book reviewer, he is currently at work on a biography of John D. Rockefeller, Sr.

Interview

Joyce Carol Oates

What made you want to be a writer?
I became a writer because I loved to write. I was writing as a child, the way many children are involved in creative activities of one kind or another, and I simply continued.

What was the subject matter of these early writings?
I wrote about my background. I lived in western New York, on a farm, which had much to do with shaping my imagination, I think.

What advice do you give to young writers today about writing fiction?
I teach creative writing and give very elementary exercises to my students, which are helpful. There isn't any use in students trying to write like Thomas Mann or William Faulkner; they just can't begin on that level. But they can begin with character sketches, with writing letters to somebody using their first-person voice, with writing dramatic monologues. It's virtually impossible to begin by writing novels.

What is the most difficult part of writing a novel?
Finding a voice for the novel is obviously the most difficult challenge. Once you have a prose style for the novel, it's much easier to write.

How do you set about creating your stories?
I do a lot of thinking. Most of my work is done in my mind. I think a good deal and then I take notes on what I've been thinking.

Where do you place your novel *Because It Is Bitter, and Because It Is My Heart* within the body of your work?
The novel is very central to my body of work, as to my experience, and was extremely difficult to write. So much of my heart seems to have gone into it, I believed afterward that I would never attempt another long novel. The first chapter alone must have been revised, sentence by sentence, as many as seventeen times. The voice was elusive—for many months, hovering just out of reach.

How did you develop the structure of this novel?
Form is very important to me; I have to divide the work into a structure that has coherence in its various parts. It's often divided in terms of years, certain spaces of time, and each space of time encompasses a development or movement in the narrative.

With *Because It Is Bitter, and Because It Is My Heart,* I wanted to write the novel in present tense, omniscient narrative, so that while we sometimes go into different people's heads, we're actually not in anybody's head; we're experiencing everything from the outside. I wanted to write it this way because I'd never written in that form. Why I chose to do it the hard way I don't know.

What do you see as the novel's theme?
It is very hard for writers to extract from the complexity of their material anything so clear as a theme; for instance, one would not want to reduce Thomas Mann's *Buddenbrooks* to the theme of decadence. I think we write to give life to experience.

I suppose my novel has much to do with the separation of races in America.

Where did your characters come from?

That's like asking a composer, "How do you write music?" It's virtually unanswerable. I think you can say they're composite characters, sometimes taken from life, but more often invented.

I knew a young black boy who is in some ways reminiscent of two of the black boys in the novel, Jinx Fairchild and his brother. The novel is actually dedicated to him. I think he's no longer living–I've been out of contact with him for more than forty years–but the novel is fiction. This boy did not commit a murder, even in self-defense.

We were students at a junior high school in Lockport, New York. Being a white girl, I was in some cases very interested in the African-American students, who were at that time called Negro students. I was brought in by school bus to the city–I was from the outside–and I think I felt that they were outsiders too, and there was a kind of alliance. I don't want to make too much of this because I didn't know this boy very well. He just had a strong personality. He was the kind of boy who could have been a leader if he hadn't been perhaps a little too rebellious.

Iris is very much based upon aspects of myself, but I did not have an alcoholic mother and father; that part is fiction. I did know someone, a very close friend, who died of alcoholism, and who is the model for Persia.

What are a writer's responsibilities, if any?

I feel that one does have responsibilities to some core of psychological realism. It may not be literal realism, but to be true to some psychological core of human experience. That's what I feel for myself. I wouldn't suggest it for everybody.

What in your creative life gives you the most pleasure?

The pleasures are so bound up with difficulties. I think the greatest pleasure is setting oneself a challenge and then working day by day, and hour by hour, to execute that challenge. It's very much like sculpting, when the sculptor has a vision in which the sculpture already exists inside the monumental piece of marble; the sculptor has to chip away and sand away to release what's already there. It's actually quite mesmerizing and challenging when one is involved in it, but the tension is so great I'm not sure it's pleasurable, or that I would even recommend the writing life for most people. To take on the contours of a difficult long novel is to invite psychic distress.

Princeton, New Jersey, 1993

JOYCE CAROL OATES is the author of more than twenty novels, as well as numerous collections of short stories, poems, essays, and plays. She received the National Book Award for her novel *Them,* and has been a finalist for three additional books, most recently *Because It Is Bitter, and Because It Is My Heart.* Ms. Oates is the Roger S. Berlind Distinguished Professor in the Humanities at Princeton University. Her most recent works are the novel *Zombie, The Perfectionist and Other Plays,* and a collection of short stories, *Will You Always Love Me?,* which will be published this year.

Censored books

Memoirs of Hecate County
EDMUND WILSON
Signet Classic
AN AMERICAN TRAGEDY
THEODORE DREISER
THE WELL OF LONELINESS
Hammond Hammond
L O L I T A
NABOKOV
TOM SAWYER
NAKED LUNCH
william s. burroughs
GROVE WEIDENFELD

U L Y S S E S
JOYCE
LADY CHATTERLEY'S LOVER
D. H. Lawrence
GROVE PRESS

HENRY MILLER TROPIC OF CANCER
Rushdie
The Satanic Verses
VIKING

The Politics of Silence

Paul Monette

This morning in *The Washington Post* there happened to be a pairing of my picture with Pat Buchanan's picture. I'm sure I'm the only one who noticed that the pictures were printed askew, so that the bottom part of mine lapped over his—almost as if I'm trying to butt in front of him. Which I am, as a matter of fact. But think of the jowl-flapping and wounded bluster at Pat's house this morning, at such an egregious example of lèse-majesté. Not to worry, Pat. I'll see to it that they don't link us romantically, even in the tabloids. We're both married men, after all, doing our leatherneck best to uphold family.

The reporter in the *Post* also notes that this could be one of my last public appearances, which is a pretty cheap way to fill a house. Have no fear. I do not expect to keel over in the next forty-five minutes. But I am reminded of a story.

My friend Bruce Vilanch is the primo comic writer in Los Angeles, the master of the one-liner, who's written material for some of the funniest people in the world. Not long ago he wrote a Vegas show for Jim Bailey, the incomparable female illusionist. Bruce flew up to Vegas for opening night, and they'd saved him a nice ringside table. This was one of those evenings where Jim wasn't going to impersonate several ladies, but just Judy Garland.

The orchestra struck up a fanfare, and Jim came strutting out dressed as Judy, belting "Swanee." And Bruce is sitting next to a couple from the Midwest, so encased in polyester they were fireproof. And the man turns to his wife and says, in some bewilderment, "I thought she was dead."

And his wife kind of pats his knee and replies with a knowing smile: "It's the daughter."

That's what I think of when people write to my publisher asking, "Is Paul Monette still alive?" No, but the daughter is.

I have titled these remarks "The Politics of Silence." A friend of mine suggested to me last week that *Becoming a Man* would have been a better book without the diatribe of the first five pages. A more seasoned writer, he seemed to imply, would have tossed those pages out before submitting the book for publication. We talked at some length about whether art should be political or not. His own sister is a novelist, a very fine one, and it was she who'd heaved my book across the room after feeling assaulted by those five pages.

I said to my friend: "Is your sister political?"

And he replied: "No, she's an artist."

This is not something I can agree to anymore. It is simply not enough to be an artist, unengaged. If you live in political times, if the lightning rod of history quivers with fire on your roof, then all art is political. And all art that is not *consciously* so partakes of the messiness of politics, if only to flee it. People still went to the opera in Nazi Germany. People still read books that were pleasant and diverting.

Robin Lane Fox, a massively learned historian of religion, says most people believe the Christian world was a fait accompli, a historical inevitability. But in point of fact, until Constantine converted to Christianity in 313, the western world was a battleground between pagans and Christians. The pagans were an urban, sophisticated class–not unlike us. They had their mysteries, and of course they had their gods, very human gods. So one of the first things the early popes did was systematically destroy pagan texts, or lock them up in monasteries. Professor Fox was able to reconstruct a semblance of the pagan world by going through ancient cemeteries reading the gravestones.

If you destroy the record, you destroy the truth.

I've learned in my adult life that the will to silence the truth is always and everywhere as strong as the truth itself. So it is a necessary fight we will always be in: those of us who struggle to understand our common truths, and those who try to erase them. The first Nazi book burning, I would have you remember, was of a gay and lesbian archive.

In that light, I think there could not be a more appropriate place to talk about censorship than the Library of Congress. Censorship is such a subtle thing. Most of it we don't even hear about, because it's done in the dark by dirty and ashamed people, by self-appointed judges who are convinced they know what's best for all of us. These are the people who always keep a match ready to start a conflagration.

We must not be lulled into a false sense of security by our First Amendment freedoms, freedoms which have never in the history of this nation been under so much attack. It is a wholly specious argument to say we are engaged in a fight between literary standards and moral standards. These matters are very specific and very concrete—the withholding of a particular book from the library shelf, the capitulation to pressure that would bar from the hungering reader books as diverse as *The Wizard of Oz, Huckleberry Finn,* and *The Catcher in the Rye.* Not to mention *The Origin of Species.*

Just this week we've been struggling with the very nub of this issue. My colleague Dorothy Allison, who was nominated for a National Book Award in fiction for an exquisite and remarkable novel called *Bastard Out of Carolina,* was abruptly canceled from giving a National Book Week speech in Oklahoma. And the most tragic thing about it is that they made their decision to censor without ever having seen the book, let alone read it. They just heard through their own grapevine that Dorothy is a lesbian poet, and suddenly it was deemed inappropriate that she address an audience that might include children.

There has been endless backing and filling and covering of tracks over this incident, with every Oklahoma library official bending backward to assure us it was all just an innocent glitch of scheduling. The schedule, you see, had been set in stone months before, and there simply wasn't room for any more authors. Really? One wonders if they would have found room for Toni Morrison or John Updike.*

For forty-five years, since the end of the war, there has been a campaign to tell people that Anne Frank never existed, that her *Diary* was a pernicious fiction, foisted on the public by the Jewish conspiracy. They haven't won yet, the rewriters of history. Anne Frank's book is still there in every library. Teenagers still get to read it. But a lot of fundamentalists don't want it in schools, because it's "obscene." And while they're at it, they don't want the Holocaust taught either, because it never happened.

Now their tactic is to check out offending books from the library and throw them away. Such has been the fate of *Heather Has Two Mommies* and *Daddy's Roommate,* both published by Alyson Press in Boston. Sasha Alyson has publicly declared that he will send these books out free to any library that wants them, but within a week they've usually vanished.

I want to say that it's difficult to speak of my fellow citizens as my enemies. I never expected to grow up with enemies.

*After much brouhaha—during which the text of this speech was considered unacceptable to be published as a pamphlet by the Library of Congress because of my remarks on the Dorothy Allison affair—a compromise was finally reached. All parties agreed to the following footnote: *The Center for the Book in the Library of Congress and the Oklahoma Department of Libraries strongly disagree with Mr. Monette's interpretation of the Dorothy Allison incident.* In the circumstances, it seems more than a little ironic that an attempt was made to censor a speech on censorship. Meanwhile, I am not expecting any flood of invitations to speak to the good people of Oklahoma.

But then, I never expected to get this far as a man, or to become so involved in the politics of my time. It's clear now that the fundamentalists' agenda of lies and hate grows daily, and it's Protestant and it's Catholic and it's Muslim and it's Jewish. It starts as a kind of lunatic fringe in each religion, till the fringe consumes the center.

It's no secret that I'm very hard on the pope, a figure of consummate evil and irresponsibility. A lot of people take umbrage at those remarks, saying "You really shouldn't be criticizing other people's faith—we still have freedom of religion in this country." Unfortunately, I think what's happened to our freedom of religion is that we're free to be nutcake fundamentalist Christians and hate everybody else. Meanwhile, no one seems capable of drawing the line between freedom of religion and the naked politics of hate.

I have great respect for anyone's relationship to his or her God, just as I have enormous esteem for priests and sisters I know who constitute a kind of resistance movement in the Church. These are the ones who believe in Liberation Theology. These are the nuns who have come out pro-choice, unleashing a witch hunt against them by the Vatican. They deserve our support and gratitude.

And as for their leaders and commandants, I've always been suspicious of their obsessive interest in other people's sex lives. People who spend all their time combating the sexuality of others suffer from a kind of sexual-compulsive personality disorder. And it's they who give tacit approval for the violence against us, whether it's a bunch of drunken louts who attack us in the streets with baseball bats or the systematic wrecking of gay kids' lives by fundamentalist parents. Many of these so-called leaders, of course, are homosexuals who can't come to terms with themselves, and they displace their own guilt and discomfort on us.

One of the most chilling things I had to write in my autobiography was that I told homophobic jokes when I was in the closet, anything to cover my own tracks. It's hard to find a corrective role model, because there really isn't a gay or lesbian spokesperson in Punditland. So many of these strutting opinion-makers—like Buchanan and Will, James Kilpatrick and William F. Buckley—have been good little Catholic boys all their lives. They were taught their intolerance in the Church of the forties and fifties, and apparently they have rigorously avoided contact with us sodomites and heathens ever since, so as not to contaminate their self-righteousness. Their fathers and their priests also believed that the Jews murdered Their Lord, but that one's been relegated to a back burner, too controversial after the Holocaust.

I would like to draw a distinction, though, between homophobia and homo-ignorance. There's much more homo-ignorance than homophobia, I think. And though it's difficult for us as a people, as a tribe, to hear the hate spewed at us, we know it's better for that hatred to be public than for it to be secret. When I speak of the politics of silence, I don't just speak for the silence of gay and lesbian people for fifteen hundred years—those rare exceptions like Whitman or Michelangelo notwithstanding. I want you to understand that that silence is as much self-imposed as imposed by our enemies. We learn the message of their hatred all too well, and we choose the closet, hoping to protect ourselves. And that very invisibility is just what our enemies want, the silence that stunts our self-esteem.

Sometimes I think that the ones who hate us can't stand the fact that we've won out over oppression. They can't stand to see us leading happy and productive lives. A joyful gay or lesbian person messes their minds profoundly. I always tell parents who are in pain after discovering their sons and daughters are gay—it's not my fault, they say; I know it's genetic, but I don't want my kid to live a pariah's life—I tell them life is difficult for everyone. The struggle for true openness and intimacy is a lifelong struggle for all of us, gay and straight alike. And besides, a difficult life brings you to the core of yourself, where you learn what justice is and how it has to be fought for. Despite all the hate and intolerance–at fever pitch these days–I would not give up a minute of the last seventeen years of being out. I'm myself now, not somebody else. I've had a full and joyous life, and that even includes the decade of AIDS. I am able to be as angry as I am at our government's indifference, as despairing as I am about how far away a cure is, and still be a happy man, because I'm so glad to be out. And because I've learned that anger against injustice is good for you. It sharpens your soul.

I consider the work I've been doing in the last six years as a kind of letter to my gay and lesbian children in the future, to them and their allies. We need our straight allies more than ever. Most of our families do the best they can to bring us up whole and make us worthy citizens. But it's a very rare person who manages to arrive at adulthood without being saddled by some form of racism or sexism or homophobia. It is our task as grownups to face those prejudices in ourselves and rethink them. The absolute minimum we can get out of such a self-examination is tolerance, one for another. We gay and lesbian people believe we should be allowed to celebrate ourselves and give back to the larger culture, make our unique contributions–but if all we can get is tolerance, we'll take it. And build on it.

We don't know what history is going to say even about this week, or where the gay and lesbian revolution is going to go. But we are a revolution that has come to be based very, very strongly on diversity. We have to fight like everyone else to be open to that diversity; but I love Urvashi Vaid's idea that it's not a matter of there being one of each on every board and every faculty and every organization. It's a matter of being *each in one*. You'll pardon my French, but it's not so hard to be politically correct. All you have to do is not be an asshole.

I want to say something about Primo Levi and implicitly about Anne Frank. For me they are the two greatest writers about the Holocaust. Primo Levi was an Italian chemist who was in Auschwitz for a long, long time. After he was liberated, he wrote about the camps for the next forty years, one book after another. The first of these is brilliant, and you wouldn't have thought he needed to do it again. But he was so convinced that history would try to lie about his experience that he had to keep writing about it to make sure he kept up with his own truth.

By the mid-fifties, commandants from the camps were beginning to publish their memoirs. "My camp wasn't like that," they said. "We had a very good arts-and-crafts program at my camp." All this surreal rethinking of history, the art of erasure—and Levi would not have that. He had too much moral force as a writer, a kind of moral fiber that I also associate with Elie Wiesel, who could face President Reagan and declare: "Mr. President, you do not belong at Bitburg. I have seen with my own eyes children thrown in the ovens. Bitburg is not your place. Your place is with the survivors, not with the SS troops."

As I remember, the White House handled that moral dilemma by making sure that when they got to Bitburg, as scheduled, everyone turned his back on the SS graves. Not a very noble or courageous statement, I'm afraid.

I repeat, the first order of business of people who would obliterate the truth is to get the books. It's all so precious and fragile. Aristotle's books wound up in the great library at Ephesus in Asia Minor, where nothing is left but an eloquent and towering facade. What happened to Aristotle's books is that Antony stole them. He sacked the library at Ephesus and brought the books to Alexandria as a tribute to Cleopatra. And you all know the rest of the story—the library at Alexandria burned, a conflagration of papyrus and waxen tablets. So we don't have a scrap of Aristotle's personal library anymore.

All so precious and fragile. The only reason we have Sappho's poems is that a copy on papyrus was rolled up and plugged in a wine jug. And the jug was stored in a cave, and by the time it was found—millennia later—there was just the neck of the jug left, with this peculiar stopper still in place. People knew enough about Sappho's writing from other sources to realize what they'd found. The blanks in Sappho's text are where the acid of the wine ate into the papyrus.

I wear a button which says I AM SALMAN RUSHDIE. I've been wearing if off and on at literary events, ever since the *fatwa* was first declared against him. He's apparently not an easy man. It's definitely not an easy book, if any of you have actually read *The Satanic Verses.* But it's so clearly art, so clearly rich in irony –but mullahs don't understand that. Rushdie has spoken fiercely and eloquently all around the world, saying, "You're *all* me, you know. If you let me go down, let me get murdered, then you're murdered too."

He's still trying to get some governments to contact Iran and use their clout to get this thing rescinded. Canada has finally agreed to speak for him. And when he came to Washington? Well, that brilliant philosopher, Marlin Fitzwater, declared, "Rushdie?" No, he's not coming to the White House. To us he's just another author on a book tour."

We will have no test for freedom of speech if the passion for it atrophies. If we are content with sound bites and TV bullshit, there will be no words to stir our hearts or even to tell us what our hearts are for. The outsider always knows that, and gay and lesbian people have always been outsiders. And always ready to fight. For a year we battled the National Endowment for the Arts, to keep it free from political manipulation.

Were I in the president's position, I don't know that I would have gone forward with the lifting of the military ban as quickly as he did. To me AIDS was the more crucial emergency that needed to be addressed. But it turns out not to matter, since either issue engages the virulence of the right wing, that frightening need to dance on our graves. The step they're going to take is to stop asking recruits, "Are you a homosexual?" Frankly, what they really need to ask is, "Are you homophobic?" Then they would know who needed some serious counseling.

I think everybody's teachable. But that is why the most pernicious of the right-wing "compromises" is to say we won't be asked our sexual orientation, but we mustn't *talk* about it either. Once again, the silence that equals death. We've had ten years of a witch-hunt, instituted by Reagan, and three hundred million dollars spent ridding the services of gay and lesbian people. *That's* the crime.

As we reclaim our history, we don't seek to exclude anybody. There's a turmoil now among certain scholars to punish great books from the past for not having the right attitude about gays and lesbians. Yet those books saved my life, even though none of the classics I read growing up ever spoke my name. Even despite that, their greatness as literature had something to speak to my heart.

We needn't tar the past for the sake of the present. As long as we understand that there's no excuse *anymore.* One of the great breakthroughs I made as a writer in the last ten years was to be able to write about lesbians. Ten years ago I silenced myself because I was so afraid I would get it wrong and come out with a stupid stereotype that wouldn't help anybody. It was my friend Katherine Forrest who said to me, "We have to populate our books with one another."

Sometimes I say to myself, "My God, we're the freest gay and lesbian people in the world." That's a stunning realization in a country where people murder us at will and pass slavery laws against us. But I have an inkling of how bad the situation is in the Third World and the Fourth World. In Muslim countries people are put to death for homosexual "behavior."

We are the crucial issue of the nineties, no doubt about *that.* We are the crucible in which it will be decided whether or not we can all come together as a people. The pie is going to get smaller and smaller, and people are going to turn more and more toward demagogues and religious crazies. *We* are the Salman Rushdies of our age. If we go down, then you all go down.

So many people have written to me since I published *Becoming a Man.* The book has a life of its own; it's more real than I am. People expect me to be as wise as *it* is, and I'm not. But so many have said it echoes their own story, women and men both, and everyone seems to conclude the same thing. We *must* be the last generation to suffer this stunted growing. We must somehow reach out to all our troubled brothers and sisters, reach out to their families, and stop the prejudice now.

There was a great recoil in this country from the tactics and language of the 1992 Republican convention. (I preferred it in the original German, as Molly Ivins acidly put it.) We are in the middle of Pat Buchanan's holy war, whether we like it or not. He and his co-religionists have a real vision of slaughtering their enemies, a regular jihad. They don't seem to understand that the Bible doesn't give them or anyone else the right to pass judgment on how a person loves.

Two can play that game, you know. Any number of scholars have read those subhuman passages from Leviticus, and they've gone back to the Aramaic, explaining over and over again that this bigotry involves a staggering amount of mistranslation. If you went with all the strictures in Leviticus, we'd all be standing on our heads in sheep dung.

For me, Jesus is patently queer. And I don't mean that as an insult to him. I'm speaking of his role as a shaman and as a healer and as a prophet. Besides, his hair is a little too well coifed, if you know what I mean. So don't throw that book in my face, because that book doesn't belong to anyone.

I get a lot of credit–poster-child credit–for being a writer with AIDS who manages to get through a lecture without keeling over. I don't know if AIDS has made me so brave as a writer. I don't know whether it has widened my heart the way witnessing the world at war widened Anne Frank's heart. Who would have thought that the greatest account of that war, the one that would sear the hearts of the future, would be written by a fourteen-year-old girl? And a fourteen-year-old who went to her death believing that people were fundamentally good. That's where I fail, much of the time.

In the thirties Picasso was asked: "What if they took everything away from you? All your paints and all your brushes and all your canvases. What would you do then? What if they put you in prison with nothing–no chalk, no nothing?"

And he said without a moment's pause: "I'd draw with my spit on the prison walls."

The winner of last year's Nobel Peace Prize, a woman named Daw Aung San Suu Kyi, has been under house arrest in Burma for years now. She went back to Burma to take care of her ailing mother. She was a free woman, married to an Oxford don. But her father was the founder of modern Burma, and when the generals took over they told her she wasn't allowed to stay and care for her mother. They wanted her *out,* so they could continue the repression and destruction of the society without any witnesses. And she said no, she wouldn't go.

She's gravely ill now from a hunger strike, and she's told the generals that she'll gladly leave. But she said, "I want all political prisoners released, and I want to walk to the airport." It's twenty miles from her prison house to the airport. And she has so rallied the spirit of her people that the generals rightly fear that the whole country would turn out to cheer her if she took that twenty-mile walk. So please think about her when you think of the politics of silence.

Or think of the Russian poet Irina Ratushinskaya. When she was in the labor camps she would write her poems on a bar of soap with a burnt matchstick. She would write a line in the soap and memorize it; and when she was sure she would never forget it, she would wash it away and go on to the next line.

The difference between having freedom as a writer and having no freedom is as narrow as the choice that the truth is important. In speech after speech Rushdie says:"What do you want a writer to be? How much will you stand up for what a writer says?"

I had one great teacher in high school, the man who more than anyone made it possible for me to write. His name was Dudley Fitts; and oh, he was such a brilliant man. He had translated the edition of Sophocles we read in senior English. He would sit in front of the class and read it in Greek while we followed along in English, and it was like being transported back to the Ancient World.

He spent a lot of time on Antigone's dilemma. If you remember, Antigone buries her brother, collecting his body from the field of battle despite the edict of Creon the king, that she will be put to death if she does so. This is the great choice in classical literature between law and conscience. Antigone chose conscience and thus chose her fate.

"O tomb, O marriage chamber," she says as she goes to her death. And the Chorus comes out to comment on what it all means. (Gary Wills could say this so much better than I.) "Isn't man wonderful?" sings the Chorus. "He longed so much to speak his heart that he taught himself language, so that what was inside him could be spoken to the world."

I was given my heart back when I came out. People say I'm too hard on myself, but if you were to read the dreary poems I wrote in my twenties, you would discover they're about nothing because they're not about me. They are not the truth.

So I guess what I would say to my gay and lesbian brothers and sisters, especially to the gay and lesbian children of the next generation, and to all our friends and allies is: Come out when you can. I know it's not easy for everybody. People misguidedly try to protect their families, or they're rightfully afraid of the impact on their jobs. I have fortunately been in a position to be way, way out on both issues—being a gay man and having AIDS.

In the meantime, even if you must keep your own life secret, hold on and support us. My friend Betty Berzon, a psychologist, says it's not enough to come out. Coming out is just the first step, a kind of outer coming out. Then we have to begin the inner coming out, looking to nourish our own battered self-esteem.

To really be a gay and lesbian citizen, you have to also give back to your community. You have to reach out and help it. Some of the people who hate us so much think we're out to indoctrinate their children. Frankly, we're trying to save their children from suicide. A third of all teen suicides are gay and lesbian, and they're all unnecessary, and we want those kids to have a chance.

To them, I try to get across the message that they're not alone.

I'll close with a thought that's been terribly important to me lately, about "The Star-Spangled Banner." Always, you understand, the right wing questions our patriotism, as if the flag were all theirs as well as the Bible. In light of which, there's a wonderful remark Kurt Vonnegut made in one of his novels, which I quoted when I won this award in November. He says "The Star-Spangled Banner" is the only national anthem in the world that ends with a question:

> Oh, say, does that star-spangled banner yet wave
> O'er the land of the free and the home of the brave?

The speaker of those words, I've always thought, is a wounded soldier who's only been able to see the flag during the long night of fighting by the glare of the rockets. And yet I also see the speaker as a refugee, clinging to his place on these shores, or just dreaming of freedom in a far-off country from which he longs to emigrate.

It makes me immensely proud as a free American that Kathleen Battle was able to sing "We Shall Overcome" on the very spot where Marian Anderson sang because the DAR threw her out of Constitution Hall. All of it under the gaze of Lincoln, who prayed that we would be worthy of the "angels of our better natures." We all stand taller because we were here on the same planet with a man as great as Justice Marshall, buried today.

I came to Washington in 1975, wide-eyed. Roger was able to get us into the Court to hear them argue the death penalty. I was an amateur student of the Court at the time, and it was literally stunning to sit in the audience and see Hugo Black and William O. Douglas and Thurgood Marshall and William Brennan and Lewis Powell and Harry Blackmun, right there in the flesh. Robert Bork was arguing for the government, as solicitor-general. Anthony Amsterdam was defense counsel, defending three black men who'd shot up a convenience store in the South. And the curious thing that I felt, watching them all day long, was that I never once thought about who was a conservative and who was a liberal. It never crossed my mind. I thought I was in the presence of philosopher-kings.

All so precious and fragile. Don't let anyone tell you that the truth can't disappear. If I believe in anything, rather than God, it's that I am part of something that goes all the way back to Antigone, and that whatever speaks the truth of our hearts can only make us stronger. Can only give us the power to counter the hate and bigotry and heal this addled world.

Just remember: You are not alone.

Washington, D.C., 1993

PAUL MONETTE is best known for his autobiographical works, *Borrowed Time: An AIDS Memoir,* and *Becoming a Man: Half a Life Story,* which won the National Book Award for nonfiction in 1992. He is also the author of six novels and three collections of poetry. Paul Monette died in 1995.

Healthy Subversions

Norman Rush

After *Mating* came out and was to my immense surprise so generously received, I found myself being asked more questions than I'm used to answering. Readers and interviewers wanted to know a lot about me. The questions fell into two categories, one easy and the other unexpectedly hard. The easy ones were variants of the question "*How* do you write?" and comprehended queries about my work habits, what writing machine I use (an antique manual typewriter), where I get my ideas, and especially where I got the idea I could write a novel in the feminine first person, and whether I had found it arduous writing a narrative without using quotation marks or giving a name to my narrator.

The array of harder questions constellated as "*Why* do you write?" or more precisely, "Why do you write this *kind* of book and why did you write this book in particular?" As I attempted to give good-faith answers to this strain of question, I realized I hadn't asked myself such questions in many years. I have always felt a compulsion to write. I've never wanted or intended to be anything but a writer. I realized that for a very long time I'd been proceeding from literary project to literary project, each one of which seemed, as I undertook it, certain to justify the fixated effort that would go into its completion. And I had always pushed a substantial backlog of projects ahead of me. It became apparent to me that the answers I was giving to the question of why I write were inadequate—not exactly evasive, but only partially responsive. So I made myself think more radically on the matter. The result of these ponderings is what I chiefly want to present here—along with answers to the easier question of how I write, as opportunities arise. Fair answers to the questions in these two columns should go some way toward filling the space controlled by the heading "The Writing Life." As I proceed, I hope to draw out the most generalizable implications of my self-interrogation. "How fascinating is that class/Whose only member is Me!" W. H. Auden wrote. I'll be unhappy if, when I conclude, those lines sum up my efforts here.

First, let me sketch the writing life I've had. Obviously it hasn't been a writing life in the sense that Henry James, say, had one. What I've had, until the last few years, is a life where—like most writers—I've managed to write in the margins of making a living and rearing a family. I've supported myself by selling used books, teaching, working in Africa as codirector (with my wife Elsa) of a Peace Corps program. I write serious fiction. "Literary novel," the industry term for the kind of novel *Mating* is, seemed like a redundancy to me on first hearing. What it means is that sales exceeding fifteen thousand copies for this kind of book would be extraordinary—and in fact the first printing of *Mating* was for just that: fifteen thousand.

I've been scribbling assiduously since I was a little boy. When I was eleven I included a feuilleton picaresque novel, *A Modern Buccaneer,* in the pages of the *Town Crier,* a newspaper I printed on a gelatin duplicator and hawked door-to-door in the Oakland, California, suburb where I grew up. Under the spell of Chesterton's Father Brown stories I created my own genius detective, Doctor Orion Curme, who physically resembled Father Brown but who was a proselytizing atheist. I sacrificed a couple of summer vacations to the writing and illustrating of twenty or so Doctor Curme stories. In junior high I wrote a novel which was the purported journal of Phra, the Phoenician, who was, incidentally, another pirate hero. I went to prison in 1951 as a war resister, wrangled a night job in the prison boilerhouse, and used the small hours to write a mock-Conradian novel about a group of high-minded adventurers losing their lives in a doomed nonviolent scheme intended to overthrow a bestial Central American dictator by the name of Larco Tur.

I believe I thought I was pioneering a promising and morally instructive new genre, that of the nonviolent thriller. When my parole was granted, after I'd spent nine months in the minimum-security prison in Tucson, it was brought home to me that I was forbidden to take any prison writings with me on release; I could take only the cards and letters that had been sent to me. I was determined to get my novel out somehow, and I terrified the very decent man who was my only authorized visitor with the proposition that on his next visit I secrete the carefully rolled-up manuscript (I wrote on both sides of each page) in the tube in the toilet-paper roll in the bathroom used both by prisoners and visitors and that he smuggle it out for me. He was a brave man and even though he was a lawyer, an officer of the court, he tremblingly agreed to do it. I'm happy to say that I reread the novel and decided it might not be worth the risk he would bear. So I copied the entire manuscript over in an even more microscopic hand on small squares of onionskin paper that I affixed in layers to the undersides of the flaplike winter scenes on my top-of-the-line Christmas cards. No one bothered, as I left, to look through my collection of rather chubby Christmas cards, nor was anyone at pains even to open up the manila envelope containing my correspondence. Back in Oakland I read my novel yet again, decided it was derivative, and threw it out. After college (Swarthmore 1956) I began to publish highly sporadically in literary quarterlies. I produced a sequence of experimental, abstract, excruciatingly self-referential novellas (all unpublished), then began to revise my approach to writing in the direction of plainness. I wrote an unpublished bildungsroman (*Equals*), began to publish in *The New Yorker*, went to Africa for five years, where it was possible only to take notes for future writing. On our return I received my first grants and fellowships, published my collection of African stories, *Whites*, in 1986, and published *Mating* in 1991. The rest, one might say, is very recent history. I've been able write full-time since 1984.

In my writing life, the intent to aim at high art emerged relatively early, not long after I'd passed through the last of my periods of self-instruction through imitation. For me, the high art of the serious novel, and of the serious short story, consists in supreme realizations of other lives–presentations of other, imagined lives, or parts of lives, variously angled, cropped, elongated, arranged with aesthetic cunning designed to elucidate the uniqueness and significance of the particular life or lives recounted. I advance this as a stipulation, for the purposes of getting on with what I have to say, although I'm always prepared to defend this contention. This presentation of selves in high art lies at the farthest point on the literary spectrum from the presentations characteristic of genre, or as they are now called, "category," novels or stories–that is, of those works that make up the vast preponderance of fiction in the modern era and whose general aim is opposite to the aims of high art, category fiction being contrived to bring the reader into repetitive and formulaic experiences, versions of the already established. After I say more about the origins of my own passion to create seriously imagined lives, I want to say something about the companion passion to enter the lives imagined in high art, the passion of the serious reader.

People become writers dedicated to high art for all kinds of reasons. Some become writers because no one will listen, or in order to propagandize, or for revenge, or to get respect, or to redo symbolically their own lives (it's amusing to note how frequently the heroes or heroines of novels turn out to be roughly the same age as their creator and to have the same syllabic count in their names as he or she does). The list looks endless. For all intending writers, there is the allure of the contest with the dead master, the invitation to demonstrate intelligence, artfulness, excellence. The correct psychological term for my impulsion toward writing would be, I think, "filial-pietistic," which refers to the carrying out of the perceived life-project of a dominant parent, the replication of it if the project has been successful or the completion of it if it has been thwarted. I think I probably began to write because my father didn't, or wouldn't. He wanted to. And it isn't quite true that he didn't. My birth in 1933 precipitated my father's abandonment of his vocation up until then as a trade-union organizer and as the California state secretary of the Socialist party. The San Francisco general strike of 1934, in which he was an activist, was the last straw for my mother, who issued an ultimatum. The scene would make a good one-act play, for which the title could be *Birth of a Salesman.* My father opened a job-printing shop, went broke at that, and then became a salesman, and finally a master-trainer of salesmen. As a boy, he had written poetry under the pseudonym Silenus Starset. As a man, for a while, he wrote Whitmanesque protest poetry that appeared in a little journal he published called *The Rebel*: this journal was circulated through an organization, the National Amateur Press Association, consisting of people who had adopted amateur status not because they had failed to get published in the usual way but apparently because they had concluded they wouldn't have been published in the usual way if they'd tried. I witnessed the devolution, as I certainly saw it, of my father's core allegiances, which took him from free thought and democratic socialism, through liberal Protestantism, and finally to the wilder shores of Rosicrucianism. As a child, I remember my father chanting John G. Neihardt's "Cry of the People" in the bathroom as he prepared to go to work:

Tremble before thy chattels,
Lords of the scheme of things!
Fighters of all earth's battles,
Ours is the might of kings!
Guided by seers and sages,
The world's heart-beat for a drum,
Snapping the chains of ages,
Out of the night we come!

Lend us no ear that pities!
Offer no almoner's hand!
Alms for the builders of cities!
When will you understand?
Down with your pride of birth
And your golden gods of trade!
A man is worth to his mother, Earth,
All that a man has made!

We are the workers and makers!
We are no longer dumb!
Tremble, O Shirkers and Takers!
Sweeping the earth—we come!
Rankled in the world-wide dawn,
Marching into the day!
The night is gone and the sword is drawn
And the scabbard is thrown away!

Toward the end of his life he would sit in the dark and chant vowel sounds in certain configurations supposed to attract angelic beings.

The trick on me was that he abandoned his original definition of himself before I had much chance to react against it, which left me with little choice but somehow to honor it. I considered the library he had assembled in early manhood to be the residue of his true self: it contained works by Zola, Erskine Caldwell, Frank Norris, James T. Farrell, Upton Sinclair, and, behind glass doors and a lock which I mastered, D. H. Lawrence, *The Sexual Life of Savages,* and racily illustrated limited editions of Rabelais and the two Defoe classics, *Moll Flanders* and *Roxana The Fortunate Mistress.* In these last two works, it has very recently occurred to me, lay the implication that a good way, maybe even the best way, for a man to write a book was in the voice of an indomitable woman. Since these books were locked up, they–I must have concluded–were the truest, because the most dangerous. (Let me not scant the contribution to the general deification of art made by my mother and her side of the family. There, it was all singing, all dancing. My mother is a lyric soprano who trained lengthily for an operatic career she was never to achieve. Her family survived the worst of the Great Depression through employment in a marionette theater organized by my Uncle Ralph. Two of my siblings have been songwriters. Among my maternal aunts and cousins are or were actors, stage directors, self-taught lute- and harpsichord-makers, modern dancers, sculptors, and puppeteers.) An odd thing is that when I began to publish, my father showed almost no interest in my work. This surprised me.

So much for the main subliminal prompting that led to my determination to become a writer. Or perhaps I should say "partly subliminal." Since it was a matter for open allusion in our family that I, personally, through being born and costing a lot to raise, had aborted my father's original more heroic mixed vocation of writing and social revolt. The allusions were rueful and not punitive in any way. We all accepted it.

Of course, once I'd begun to write, and as I moved deeper into the world of books, all the usual impulses that will sustain the drive to write declared themselves. Increasingly, I wanted to write because literature meant liberation to me, liberation from the thrall of my own personal cast of demons. And what nobler life-objective could there be than qualifying myself as an affiliate of those who, from their resting places in the stacks of the

Melrose Library, had helped me convert alienation into productive autonomy?

The conviction that I could add something distinctly my own to the deep appreciation of lives lived in my time grew not with the success of my literary efforts but with the strengthening both of my craft and of my sense that subtle yet enormous changes were coming virtually unremarked into the way we live now. Being in Africa for five years drastically intensified all my impulses to capture life as I saw it there, pursuant to the sudden shift in the relationship between figure and ground that finding oneself "altogether elsewhere" (W. H. Auden) so often yields.

Finally, beyond the intent commandingly to present lives which in new ways summarize and embody previously unevoked aesthetic and moral themes and conclusions, there is another aspiration, which is one day to find that one's work, through luck or inspiration, has, in the manner of a fractal, managed to condense truths about the condition of Ïhuman that transcend the boundaries of time and place within which one has chosen consciously to work. This is a prize that is almost never won.

I'd like now to consider the civic dimensions of the act of writing seriously, of writing serious fiction in particular, and to look concurrently at the worsening siege conditions affecting the place where all writing is done. Several tendencies in our culture are grimly menacing to the future of the book, all books, not excluding the most narrowly technical and utilitarian. Most conspicuously, there is the persistence of illiteracy and the growth of paraliteracy. The statistics are oppressive–thirty-six million adult Americans reading at an eighth-grade level or below–and the causes track back to defects in formal education, to deterioration in educative processes within families, and to the desk-killing effects flowing from the rise of competitive visual media–the electronic media preeminently, with their commercially driven bias toward shallow amusement, repetition (again), interruptability, generic amiability, amnesia, and the micro-division of units of presentation. Additionally, the forces favoring censorship are growing bolder, drawing sustenance from the old and new political and religious fundamentalisms currently asserting themselves. And then there is the sheer, brute crowding out of books by cultural substitutes whose use requires less energy and less attention. In this connection, I quote briefly from a recent study, Neil Postman's *Amusing Ourselves to Death*: "From Erasmus in the sixteenth century to Elizabeth Eisenstein in the twentieth, almost every scholar who has grappled with the question of what reading does to one's habits of mind has concluded that the process encourages rationality; that the sequential, propositional character of the written word fosters what Walter Ong calls the "analytic management of knowledge."

Nasty synergies emerge. Negative tendencies reinforce one another over time. Illiteracy cohabits with television, even as television–recent research shows–weakens the ability of young brains to access the riches encoded in text. Political discourse suffers in all this, and not only because language and thus expressive competence are in decline; worse, the dominance of visual media of the kind we seem to have created for ourselves leads to translocation of political contestation away from argument and toward a witless competition among images. A muffled panic in the public results, manifesting itself sometimes as apathy, sometimes as support for various fundamentalisms–religious, political, cultural-political, as in identity politics–whose essential maneuver is to make the world more agreeable by curtailing the flow of cultural material disquieting to their followerships. It hardly needs to be emphasized that this weakening of political discourse, and thereby of the self-renewing capacities of our democracy, comes at a bad time. We seem to be entering what looks very much like a general crisis of the present global dispensation tion, extending even to the natural systems on which social survival is premised. In defending books, we defend the critical powers potentiated by them. None of the above is news, really, but it's important that we remain aware of the gravity of our predicament. Consider how difficult it seems to be for even those economic entities like newspapers of record and weekly news magazines—entities directly dependent on a continuing, broadly based public capacity to read competently—how difficult it seems to be for them to grasp the degree to which they abet the tendencies undoing them: *The New York Times* has recently eliminated the book review column in its Saturday editions, and both *Time* and *Newsweek* now occasionally entirely skip coverage of the world of books. Throughout the daily press the length and number of book reviews are steadily declining, and the process of reviewing is yielding almost everywhere to pressures to make stars or letter-grades or some other reductive ranking device as part of the review.

In conclusion, I'd like to concentrate on the particular civic functions of serious fiction, and to link myself with those who identify the drive to read it and write it as fundamentally ethical in character. Why is the serious reader drawn again and again to the interminable parade of imagined lives kept marching forth by writers and publishers? We are, I think, seeing some elusive thing or outcome, something answering to a need stronger than the voyeurism or curiosity or desire for distraction that may lead us to any book initially.

I think we would like to love our species, if we could. And I think that if we are even a little educated, we know how limited is our individual ability to see around or through the influences that have shaped our powers to understand the world and ourselves. We resemble, individually, sufferers from agnosia, a perceptual disorder whose victims are able to identify the properties of an object without being able to recognize what the object is. We know that we each arrive in the world wearing the infinitely fine net custom-woven for us by the Fates, a net whose knots tighten each time we step off the track that has been preselected for us. We can love our species because we are ordered to by the spiritual director of our choice, or we can attempt, by passing through the alternative lives serious fiction brings us, to assemble a truer composite of what we are, with the intent of discovering, in the process, to what degree we should enlarge or qualify the baffled unformed sympathy we begin with. In stories or the novel, we are privileged to enjoy the least constrained representation of life achievable in any communicative form. Expository writing can't help but declare its viewpoint, and we normally know the bearing of the real lives presented in biography and autobiography before we begin, because the reputation of the subject alerts us. In serious fiction, we are able to enter disarmed and to open ourselves to the healthy subversions produced by the truth told excessively and beautifully and from vantage points different from our own and different from one another. Truth is a product of collaboration. We writers know it, and that's why, despite the ineliminably rivalrous atmosphere in which we work, we feel ourselves uplifted–for a time, anyway–by the occasional triumphs of our peers in seizing and displaying a life that tells us things no life has ever told us before.

These are large claims for literature, I know, but the iron compulsion of the different fundamentalisms to suppress or stigmatize whole classes of imagined lives suggests to me that I'm correct. Proletcult, a mass movement in the Russia of 1919, dismissed all literature produced before 1917 as bourgeois–Chekhov, Turgenev, Tolstoy, Pushkin, no exceptions. The local Proletcult chapter in Tambov planned to burn all the books in the libraries "in the belief that the shelves would refill on the first of the new year with nothing but proletarian works," as Richard Stites records. In Nazi Germany, as we all know, it was the test of Aryanness that imagined lives had to pass. We have had the Index Librorum Prohibitorum and we have with us today the international death sentence pronounced on Salman Rushdie by the Ayatollah Ruhollah Khomeini, whose ascent to power Michel Foucault, in a spectacular display of agnosia, welcomed as "the eruption of the sacred into modernity."

I hope I've shed some light on the enterprise of writing serious fiction. And I hope I've suggested persuasively that serious fiction has utilities we ignore at our own peril.

Philadelphia, Pennsylvania, 1992

NORMAN RUSH is the author of a collection of short stories, *Whites,* a National Book Award finalist, and a novel, *Mating,* which won the National Book Award for Fiction in 1991. He is at work on a new novel, entitled *Mortals.*

National Book Award Winners

1950–1994

1950

FICTION: Nelson Algren–*The Man with the Golden Arm*

NONFICTION: Ralph L. Rusk–*Ralph Waldo Emerson*

POETRY: William Carlos Williams–*Paterson: Book III* and *Selected Poems*

1951

FICTION: William Faulkner–*The Collected Stories*

NONFICTION: Newton Arvin–*Herman Melville*

POETRY: Wallace Stevens–*The Auroras of Autumn*

1952

FICTION: James Jones–*From Here to Eternity*

NONFICTION: Rachel Carson–*The Sea Around Us*

POETRY: Marianne Moore–*Collected Poems*

1953

FICTION: Ralph Ellison–*Invisible Man*

NONFICTION: Bernard A. DeVoto–*The Course of an Empire*

POETRY: Archibald MacLeish–*Collected Poems 1917–1952*

1954

FICTION: Saul Bellow–*The Adventures of Augie March*

NONFICTION: Bruce Catton–*A Stillness at Appomattox*

POETRY: Conrad Aiken–*Collected Poems*

1955

FICTION: William Faulkner–*A Fable*

NONFICTION: Joseph Wood Krutch–*The Measure of Man*

POETRY: Wallace Stevens–*Collected Poems*

1956

FICTION: John O'Hara–*Ten North Frederick*

NONFICTION: Herbert Kubly–*An American in Italy*

POETRY: W. H. Auden–*The Shield of Achilles*

1957

FICTION: Wright Morris–*The Field of Vision*

NONFICTION: George F. Kennan–*Russia Leaves the War*

POETRY: Richard Wilbur–*Things of This World*

1958

FICTION: John Cheever–*The Wapshot Chronicle*

NONFICTION: Catherine Drinker Bowen–*The Lion and the Throne*

POETRY: Robert Penn Warren–*Promises: Poems, 1954–1956*

1959

FICTION: Bernard Malamud–*The Magic Barrel*

NONFICTION: J. Christopher Herold–*Mistress to an Age: A Life of Madame de Staël*

POETRY: Theodore Roethke–*Words for the Wind*

1960

FICTION: Philip Roth–*Goodbye, Columbus*

NONFICTION: Richard Ellmann–*James Joyce*

POETRY: Robert Lowell–*Life Studies*

1961

FICTION: Conrad Richter–*The Waters of Kronos*

NONFICTION: William L. Shirer–*The Rise and Fall of the Third Reich*

POETRY: Randall Jarrell–*The Woman at the Washington Zoo*

1962

FICTION: Walker Percy–*The Moviegoer*

NONFICTION: Lewis Mumford–*The City in History: Its Origins, Its Transformations and Its Prospects*

POETRY: Alan Dugan–*Poems*

1963

FICTION: J. F. Powers–*Morte D'Urban*

NONFICTION: Leon Edel–*Henry James, Vol. II: The Conquest of London; Henry James, Vol. III: The Middle Years*

POETRY: William Stafford–*Traveling through the Dark*

1964

FICTION: John Updike–*The Centaur*

ARTS & LETTERS: Aileen Ward–*John Keats: The Making of a Poet*

HISTORY & BIOGRAPHY: William H. McNeill–*The Rise of the West: A History of the Human Community*

SCIENCE, PHILOSOPHY & RELIGION: Christopher Tunnard & Boris Pushkarev–*Man-Made America*

POETRY: John Crowe Ransom–*Selected Poems*

1965

ARTS & LETTERS: Eleanor Clark–*The Oysters of Locmariaquer*

FICTION: Saul Bellow–*Herzog*

HISTORY & BIOGRAPHY: Louis Fischer–*The Life of Lenin*

POETRY: Theodore Roethke–*The Far Field*

SCIENCE, PHILOSOPHY & RELIGION: Norbert Wiener–*God and Golem, Inc: A Comment on Certain Points Where Cybernetics Impinges on Religion*

1966

ARTS & LETTERS: Janet Flanner–*Paris Journal: 1944–1965*

FICTION: Katherine Anne Porter–*Collected Stories*

HISTORY & BIOGRAPHY: Arthur M. Schlesinger, Jr.–*A Thousand Days*

POETRY: James Dickey–*Buckdancer's Choice: Poems*

1967

ARTS & LETTERS: Justin Kaplan–*Mr. Clemens and Mark Twain: A Biography*

FICTION: Bernard Malamud–*The Fixer*

HISTORY & BIOGRAPHY: Peter Gay–*The Enlightenment, Vol. I: An Interpretation of the Rise of Modern Paganism*

POETRY: James Merrill–*Nights and Days*

SCIENCE, PHILOSOPHY & RELIGION: Oscar Lewis–*La Vida*

TRANSLATION: Gregory Rabassa–Julio Cortázar's *Hopscotch*
Willard Trask–Casanova's *History of My Life*

1968

ARTS & LETTERS: William Troy–*Selected Essays*

FICTION: Thornton Wilder–*The Eighth Day*

HISTORY & BIOGRAPHY: George F. Kennan–*Memoirs: 1925–1950*

POETRY: Robert Bly–*The Light Around the Body*

SCIENCE, PHILOSOPHY & RELIGION: Jonathan Kozol–*Death at an Early Age*

TRANSLATION: Howard & Edna Hong–Søren Kierkegaard's *Journals and Papers*

1969

ART & LETTERS: Norman Mailer–*The Armies of the Night: History as a Novel, The Novel as History*

CHILDREN'S LITERATURE: Meindert DeJong–*Journey from Peppermint Street*

FICTION: Jerzy Kosinski–*Steps*

HISTORY & BIOGRAPHY: Winthrop D. Jordan–*White over Black: American Attitudes Toward the Negro, 1550–1812*

POETRY: John Berryman–*His Toy, His Dream, His Rest*

THE SCIENCES: Robert J. Lifton–*Death in Life: Survivors of Hiroshima*

TRANSLATION: William Weaver–Italo Calvino's *Cosmicomics*

1970

ARTS & LETTERS: Lillian Hellman–*An Unfinished Woman: A Memoir*

CHILDREN'S BOOKS: Isaac Bashevis Singer–*A Day of Pleasure: Stories of a Boy Growing Up in Warsaw*

FICTION: Joyce Carol Oates–*Them*

HISTORY & BIOGRAPHY: T. Harry Williams–*Huey Long*

PHILOSOPHY & RELIGION: Erik H. Erikson–*Gandhi's Truth: On the Origins of Militant Nonviolence*

POETRY: Elizabeth Bishop–*The Complete Poems*

TRANSLATION: Ralph Manheim–Céline's *Castle to Castle*

1971

ARTS & LETTERS: Francis Steegmuller–*Cocteau: A Biography*

CHILDREN'S BOOKS: Lloyd Alexander–*The Marvelous Misadventures of Sebastian*

FICTION: Saul Bellow–*Mr. Sammler's Planet*

HISTORY & BIOGRAPHY: James MacGregor Burns–*Roosevelt: The Soldier of Freedom*

POETRY: Mona Van Duyn–*To See, To Take*

THE SCIENCES: Raymond Phineas Sterns–*Science in the British Colonies of America*

TRANSLATION: Frank Jones–Bertolt Brecht's *Saint Joan of the Stockyards*
Edward G. Seidensticker–Yasunari Kawabata's *The Sound of the Mountain*

1972

ARTS & LETTERS: Charles Rosen–*The Classical Style: Haydn, Mozart, Beethoven*

BIOGRAPHY: Joseph P. Lash–*Eleanor and Franklin: The Story of Their Relationship, Based on Eleanor Roosevelt's Private Papers*

CHILDREN'S BOOKS: Donald Barthelme–*The Slightly Irregular Fire Engine or The Hithering Thithering Djinn*

CONTEMPORARY AFFAIRS: Stewart Brand, *ed.*–*The Last Whole Earth Catalogue*

FICTION: Flannery O'Connor–*The Complete Stories of Flannery O'Connor*

HISTORY: Allan Nevins–*Ordeal of the Union, Vols. VII & VIII: The Organized War, 1863–1864* and *The Organized War to Victory*

PHILOSOPHY & RELIGION: Martin E. Marty–*Righteous Empire: The Protestant Experience in America*

POETRY: Howard Moss–*Selected Poems*
Frank O'Hara–*The Collected Poems*

THE SCIENCES: George L. Small–*The Blue Whale*

TRANSLATION: Austryn Wainhouse–Jacques Monod's *Chance and Necessity*

1973

ARTS & LETTERS: Arthur M. Wilson–*Diderot*

BIOGRAPHY: James Thomas Flexner–*George Washington, Vol. IV: Anguish and Farewell, 1793–1799*

CHILDREN'S BOOKS: Ursula K. LeGuin–*The Farthest Shore*

CONTEMPORARY AFFAIRS: Frances FitzGerald–*Fire in the Lake: The Vietnamese and the Americans in Vietnam*

FICTION: John Barth–*Chimera*
John Williams–*Augustus*

HISTORY: Robert Manson Myers–*The Children of Pride*
Isaiah Trunk–*Judenrat*

PHILOSOPHY & RELIGION: S. E. Ahlstrom–*A Religious History of the American People*

POETRY: A. R. Ammons–*Collected Poems, 1951–1971*

THE SCIENCES: George B. Schaller–*The Serengeti Lion: A Study of Predator–Prey Relations*

TRANSLATION: Allen Mandelbaum–*The Aeneid of Virgil*

1974

ART & LETTERS: Pauline Kael–*Deeper into the Movies*

BIOGRAPHY: John Clive–*Macaulay: The Shaping of the Historian*
Douglas Day–*Malcolm Lowry: A Biography*

CHILDREN'S BOOKS: Eleanor Cameron–*The Court of the Stone Children*

CONTEMPORARY AFFAIRS: Murray Kempton–*The Briar Patch*

FICTION: Thomas Pynchon–*Gravity's Rainbow*
Isaac Bashevis Singer–*A Crown of Feathers and Other Stories*

HISTORY: John Clive–*Macaulay: The Shaping of the Historian*

PHILOSOPHY & RELIGION: Maurice Natanson–*Edmund Husserl: Philosopher of Infinite Tasks*

POETRY: Allen Ginsberg–*The Fall of America: Poems of These States 1965–1971*
Adrienne Rich–*Diving into the Wreck: Poems 1971–1972*

THE SCIENCES: S. E. Luria–*Life: The Unfinished Experiment*

TRANSLATION: Karen Brazell–*The Confessions of Lady Nijo*
Helen R. Lane–Octavio Paz's *Alternating Current*
Jackson Matthews–Paul Valéry's *Monsieur Teste*

1975

ARTS & LETTERS: Roger Shattuck–*Marcel Proust*
Lewis Thomas–*The Lives of a Cell: Notes of a Biology Watcher*

BIOGRAPHY: Richard B. Sewall–*The Life of Emily Dickinson*

CHILDREN'S BOOKS: Virginia Hamilton–*M. C. Higgins the Great*

CONTEMPORARY AFFAIRS: Theodore Rosengarten–*All God's Dangers: The Life of Nate Shaw*

FICTION: Robert Stone–*Dog Soldiers*
Thomas Williams–*The Hair of Harold Roux*

HISTORY: Bernard Bailyn–*The Ordeal of Thomas Hutchinson*

PHILOSOPHY & RELIGION: Robert Nozick–*Anarchy, State and Utopia*

POETRY: Marilyn Hacker–*Presentation Piece*

THE SCIENCES: Silvano Arieti–*Interpretation of Schizophrenia*
Lewis Thomas–*The Lives of a Cell: Notes of a Biology Watcher*

TRANSLATION: Anthony Kerrigan–Miguel D. Unamuno's *The Agony of Christianity* and *Essays on Faith*

1976

ARTS & LETTERS: Paul Fussell–*The Great War and Modern Memory*

CHILDREN'S LITERATURE: Walter D. Edmonds–*Bert Breen's Barn*

CONTEMPORARY AFFAIRS: Michael J. Arlen–*Passage to Ararat*

FICTION: William Gaddis–*JR*

HISTORY & BIOGRAPHY: David Brion Davis–*The Problem of Slavery in the Age of Revolution, 1770–1823*

POETRY: John Ashbery–*Self-Portrait in a Convex Mirror*

1977

BIOGRAPHY & AUTOBIOGRAPHY: W. A. Swanberg–*Norman Thomas: The Last Idealist*

CHILDREN'S LITERATURE: Katherine Paterson–*The Master Puppeteer*

CONTEMPORARY THOUGHT: Bruno Bettelheim–*The Uses of Enchantment: The Meaning and Importance of Fairy Tales*

FICTION: Wallace Stegner–*The Spectator Bird*

HISTORY: Irving Howe–*World of Our Fathers*

POETRY: Richard Eberhart–*Selected Poems, 1930–1976*

TRANSLATION: Li-Li Ch'en–Master Tung's *Western Chamber Romance*

1978

BIOGRAPHY & AUTOBIOGRAPHY: W. Jackson Bate–*Samuel Johnson*

CHILDREN'S LITERATURE: Judith Kohl & Herbert Kohl–*The View from the Oak*

CONTEMPORARY THOUGHT: Gloria Emerson–*Winners & Losers*

FICTION: Mary Lee Settle–*Blood Ties*

HISTORY: David McCullough–*The Path Between the Seas: The Creation of the Panama Canal 1870–1914*

POETRY: Howard Nemerov–*The Collected Poems*

TRANSLATION: Richard Winston & Clara Winston–Uwe George's *In the Deserts of This Earth*

1979

BIOGRAPHY & AUTOBIOGRAPHY: Arthur M. Schlesinger, Jr.–*Robert Kennedy and His Times*

CHILDREN'S LITERATURE: Katherine Paterson–*The Great Gilly Hopkins*

CONTEMPORARY THOUGHT: Peter Matthiessen–*The Snow Leopard*

FICTION: Tim O'Brien–*Going After Cacciato*

HISTORY: Richard Beale Davis–*Intellectual Life in the Colonial South, 1585–1763*

POETRY: James Merrill–*Mirabell: Books of Number*

TRANSLATION: Clayton Eshleman & José Rubin Barcia–César Vallejo's *The Complete Posthumous Poetry*

1980

AUTOBIOGRAPHY (HARDCOVER): Lauren Bacall–*Lauren Bacall by Myself*

AUTOBIOGRAPHY (PAPERBACK): Malcolm Cowley–*And I Worked at the Writer's Trade: Chapters of Literary History 1918–1978*

BIOGRAPHY (HARDCOVER): Edmund Morris–*The Rise of Theodore Roosevelt*

BIOGRAPHY (PAPERBACK): A. Scott Berg–*Max Perkins: Editor of Genius*

CHILDREN'S BOOKS (HARDCOVER): Joan W. Blos–*A Gathering of Days: A New England Girl's Journal*

CHILDREN'S BOOKS (PAPERBACK): Madeleine L'Engle–*A Swiftly Tilting Planet*

CURRENT INTEREST (HARDCOVER): Julia Child–*Julia Child and More Company*

CURRENT INTEREST (PAPERBACK): Christopher Lasch–*The Culture of Narcissism*

FICTION (HARDCOVER): William Styron–*Sophie's Choice*

FICTION (PAPERBACK): John Irving–*The World According to Garp*

FIRST NOVEL: William Wharton–*Birdy*

GENERAL NONFICTION (HARDCOVER): Tom Wolfe–*The Right Stuff*

GENERAL NONFICTION (PAPERBACK): Peter Matthiessen–*The Snow Leopard*

GENERAL REFERENCE BOOKS (HARDCOVER): Elder Witt, *ed.*–*Congressional Quarterly's Guide to the U.S. Supreme Court*

GENERAL REFERENCE BOOKS (PAPERBACK): Tim Brooks & Earle Marsh–*The Complete Directory of Prime Time Network TV Shows: 1946–Present*

HISTORY (HARDCOVER): Henry A. Kissinger–*The White House Years*

HISTORY (PAPERBACK): Barbara W. Tuchman–*A Distant Mirror: The Calamitous Fourteenth Century*

MYSTERY (HARDCOVER): John D. MacDonald–*The Green Ripper*

MYSTERY (PAPERBACK): William F. Buckley, Jr.–*Stained Glass*

POETRY: Philip Levine–*Ashes*

RELIGION/INSPIRATION (HARDCOVER): Elaine Pagels–*The Gnostic Gospels*

RELIGION/INSPIRATION (PAPERBACK): Sheldon Vanauken–*A Severe Mercy*

SCIENCE (HARDCOVER): Douglas Hofstadter–*Godel, Escher, Bach: An Eternal Golden Braid*

SCIENCE (PAPERBACK): Gary Zukav–*The Dancing Wu Li Masters: An Overview of the New Physics*

SCIENCE FICTION (HARDCOVER): Frederik Pohl–*Jem*

SCIENCE FICTION (PAPERBACK): Walter Wangerin, Jr.–*The Book of the Dun Cow*

TRANSLATION: William Arrowsmith–Cesare Pavese's *Hard Labor*
Jane Gary Harris & Constance Link–Osip E. Mandelstam's *Complete Critical Prose and Letters*

WESTERN: Louis L'Amour–*Bendigo Shafter*

1981

AUTOBIOGRAPHY/BIOGRAPHY (HARDCOVER): Justin Kaplan–*Walt Whitman*

AUTOBIOGRAPHY/BIOGRAPHY (PAPERBACK): Deirdre Bair–*Samuel Beckett*

CHILDREN'S BOOKS, FICTION (HARDCOVER): Betsy Byars–*The Night Swimmers*

CHILDREN'S BOOKS, FICTION (PAPERBACK): Beverly Cleary–*Ramona and Her Mother*

CHILDREN'S BOOKS, NONFICTION (HARDCOVER): Alison Cragin Herzig & Jane Lawrence Mali–*Oh, Boy! Babies*

FICTION (HARDCOVER): Wright Morris–*Plains Song*

FICTION (PAPERBACK): John Cheever–*The Stories*

FIRST NOVEL: Ann Arensberg–*Sister Wolf*

GENERAL NONFICTION (HARDCOVER): Maxine Hong Kingston–*China Men*

GENERAL NONFICTION (PAPERBACK): Jane Kramer–*The Last Cowboy*

HISTORY (HARDCOVER): John Boswell–*Christianity, Social Tolerance and Homosexuality*

HISTORY (PAPERBACK): Leon F. Litwak–*Been in the Storm so Long: The Aftermath of Slavery*

POETRY: Lisel Mueller–*The Need to Hold Still*

SCIENCE (HARDCOVER): Stephen Jay Gould–*The Panda's Thumb: More Reflections in Natural History*

SCIENCE (PAPERBACK): Lewis Thomas–*The Medusa and the Snail*

TRANSLATION: Francis Steegmuller–*The Letters of Gustave Flaubert*
John E. Woods–Arno Schmidt's *Evening Edged in Gold*

1982

AUTOBIOGRAPHY/BIOGRAPHY (HARDCOVER): David McCullough–*Mornings on Horseback*

AUTOBIOGRAPHY/BIOGRAPHY (PAPERBACK): Ronald Steel–*Walter Lippmann and the American Century*

CHILDREN'S BOOKS, FICTION (HARDCOVER): Lloyd Alexander–*Westmark*

CHILDREN'S BOOKS, FICTION (PAPERBACK): Ouida Sebestyen–*Words by Heart*

CHILDREN'S BOOKS, NONFICTION: Susan Bonners–*A Penguin Year*

CHILDREN'S BOOKS, PICTURE BOOKS (HARDCOVER): Maurice Sendak–*Outside Over There*

CHILDREN'S BOOKS, PICTURE BOOKS (PAPERBACK): Peter Spier–*Noah's Ark*

FICTION (HARDCOVER): John Updike–*Rabbit Is Rich*

FICTION (PAPERBACK): William Maxwell–*So Long, See You Tomorrow*

FIRST NOVEL: Robb Forman Dew–*Dale Loves Sophie to Death*

GENERAL NONFICTION (HARDCOVER): Tracy Kidder–*The Soul of a New Machine*

GENERAL NONFICTION (PAPERBACK): Victor S. Navasky–*Naming Names*

HISTORY (HARDCOVER): Father Peter John Powell–*People of the Sacred Mountain: A History of the Northern Cheyenne Chiefs and Warrior Societies, 1830–1879*

HISTORY (PAPERBACK): Robert Wohl–*The Generation of 1914*

POETRY: William Bronk–*Life Supports: New and Collected Poems*

SCIENCE (HARDCOVER): Donald C. Johanson & Maitland A. Edey–*Lucy: The Beginnings of Humankind*

SCIENCE (PAPERBACK): Fred Alan Wolf–*Taking the Quantum Leap: The New Physics for Nonscientists*

TRANSLATION: Robert Lyons Danly–Higuchi Ichiyo's *In the Shade of Spring Leaves*
Ian Hideo Levy–*The Ten Thousand Leaves: A Translation of* The Man'Yoshu

1983

AUTOBIOGRAPHY/BIOGRAPHY (HARDCOVER): Judith Thurman–*Isak Dinesen: The Life of a Storyteller*

AUTOBIOGRAPHY/BIOGRAPHY (PAPERBACK): James R. Mellow–*Nathaniel Hawthorne in His Time*

CHILDREN'S FICTION (HARDCOVER): Jean Fritz–*Homesick: My Own Story*

CHILDREN'S FICTION (PAPERBACK): Paula Fox–*A Place Apart*
Joyce Carol Thomas–*Marked by Fire*

CHILDREN'S BOOKS, NONFICTION: James Cross Giblin–*Chimney Sweeps*

CHILDREN'S PICTURE BOOKS (HARDCOVER): Barbara Cooney–*Miss Rumphius*
William Steig–*Doctor De Soto*

CHILDREN'S PICTURE BOOKS (PAPERBACK): Mary Ann Hoberman; Betty Fraser, *ill.*–*A House Is a House for Me*

FICTION (HARDCOVER): Alice Walker–*The Color Purple*

FICTION (PAPERBACK): Eudora Welty–*Collected Stories*

FIRST NOVEL: Gloria Naylor–*The Women of Brewster Place*

GENERAL NONFICTION (HARDCOVER): Fox Butterfield–*China: Alive in the Bitter Sea*

GENERAL NONFICTION (PAPERBACK): James Fallows–*National Defense*

HISTORY (HARDCOVER): Alan Brinkley–*Voices of Protest: Huey Long, Father Coughlin and the Great Depression*

HISTORY (PAPERBACK): Frank E. Manuel & Fritzie P. Manuel–*Utopian Thought in the Western World*

ORIGINAL PAPERBACK: Lisa Goldstein–*The Red Magician*

POETRY: Galway Kinnell–*Selected Poems*
Charles Wright–*Country Music: Selected Early Poems*

SCIENCE (HARDCOVER): Abraham Pais–*"Subtle is the Lord...": The Science and Life of Albert Einstein*

SCIENCE (PAPERBACK): Philip J. Davis & Reuben Hersh–*The Mathematical Experience*

TRANSLATION: Richard Howard–Charles Baudelaire's *Les Fleurs du Mal*

1984

FICTION: Ellen Gilchrist–*Victory over Japan: A Book of Stories*

FIRST WORK OF FICTION: Harriet Doerr–*Stones for Ibarra*

NONFICTION: Robert V. Remini–*Andrew Jackson & the Course of American Democracy, 1833–1845*

1985

FICTION: Don DeLillo–*White Noise*

FIRST WORK OF FICTION: Bob Shacochis–*Easy in the Islands*

NONFICTION: J. Anthony Lukas–*Common Ground: A Turbulent Decade in the Lives of Three American Families*

1986

FICTION: E. L. Doctorow–*World's Fair*

NONFICTION: Barry Lopez–*Arctic Dreams*

1987

FICTION: Larry Heinemann–*Paco's Story*

NONFICTION: Richard Rhodes–*The Making of the Atom Bomb*

1988

FICTION: Pete Dexter–*Paris Trout*

NONFICTION: Neil Sheehan–*A Bright Shining Lie: John Paul Vann and America in Vietnam*

1989

FICTION: John Casey–*Spartina*

NONFICTION: Thomas L. Friedman–*From Beirut to Jerusalem*

1990

FICTION: Charles Johnson–*Middle Passage*

NONFICTION: Ron Chernow–*The House of Morgan: An American Banking Dynasty and the Rise of Modern Finance*

1991

FICTION: Norman Rush–*Mating*

NONFICTION: Orlando Patterson–*Freedom*

POETRY: Philip Levine–*What Work Is*

1992

FICTION: Cormac McCarthy–*All the Pretty Horses*

NONFICTION: Paul Monette–*Becoming a Man: Half a Life Story*

POETRY: Mary Oliver–*New & Selected Poems*

1993

FICTION: E. Annie Proulx–*The Shipping News*

NONFICTION: Gore Vidal–*United States: Essays 1952–1992*

POETRY: A. R. Ammons–*Garbage*

1994

FICTION: William Gaddis–*A Frolic of His Own*

NONFICTION: Sherwin B. Nuland–*How We Die: Reflections on Life's Final Chapter*

POETRY: James Tate–*A Worshipful Company of Fletchers*

Acknowledgments

As a nonprofit organization with the ambitious mission to raise the cultural value of great American writing, the National Book Foundation has come to depend in the first years of its institutional life upon many generous friends and supporters in the publishing industry.

The informing idea for this volume was first proposed by Alberto A. Vitale, chairman, president and CEO of Random House, Inc., and a long-time foundation board member. His determined energies kept the project moving forward from inspired concept to finished book.

The board of directors and staff of the foundation also wish to express their deep gratitude to the other members of the Random House family for their editorial creativity and persistence in making *The Writing Life* anthology a reality: Harry Evans, Helen Morris, Wynn Dan, Elsa Burt, Jean-Isabel McNutt, Della Mancuso, and Stacy Rockwood; and to the vendors who have generously donated their goods and services for this project: Phoenix Color Corp, Quebecor Printing Book Group, and Rainy River Forest Products.

Grateful acknowledgment is made to the following authors and publishers for permission to use the following material:

LOUIS BEGLEY: Interview with National Book Foundation regarding "The Writing Life." Used by permission.

JOHN CASEY: "Dogma." Copyright © by John D. Casey. Used by permission.

RON CHERNOW: "Stubborn Facts and Fickle Realities." Copyright © by Ron Chernow. Used by permission.

THOMAS L. FRIEDMAN: "Beirut to Jerusalem to Washington." Copyright © by Thomas L. Friedman. Used by permission.

GAIL GODWIN: "Rituals and Readiness: Getting Ready to Write." Copyright © by Gail Godwin. Used by permission.

HARCOURT BRACE & COMPANY: "The Politics of Silence" from *Last Watch of the Night* by Paul Monette. Copyright © 1994, 1993 by Paul Monette, Trustee, and his successor Trustee/s of the Monette/Horwitz trust u/i 3/12/92. Reprinted by permission of Harcourt Brace & Company.

ALFRED A. KNOPF, INC.: "Entering Poetry" from *The Bread of Time* by Philip Levine. Copyright © 1994 by Philip Levine. Reprinted by permission of Alfred A. Knopf, Inc.

R.W.B. LEWIS: "Writers at the Century's Turn." Copyright © by R.W.B. Lewis. Used by permission.

J. ANTHONY LUKAS: Interview with National Book Foundation regarding "The Writing Life." Used by permission.

DAVID McCULLOUGH: Interview with National Book Foundation regarding "The Writing Life." Used by permission.

GLORIA NAYLOR: "The Love of Books." Copyright © by Gloria Naylor. Used by permission.

JOYCE CAROL OATES: Interview with National Book Foundation regarding "The Writing Life." Copyright © by The Ontario Review, Inc. Used by permission.

E. ANNIE PROULX: "The Book Tour." Copyright © by E. Annie Proulx. Used by permission.

MARILYNNE ROBINSON: Interview with National Book Foundation regarding "The Writing Life." Used by permission.

NORMAN RUSH: "Healthy Subversions." Copyright © by Norman Rush. Used by permission.

SANDRA SCOFIELD: "Parkside: Writing from Love and Grief and Fear." Copyright © by Sandra Scofield. Used by permission.

BOB SHACOCHIS: "Breathing Space." Copyright © 1995 by Bob Shacochis. Used by permission.

UNIVERSITY OF NEBRASKA PRESS: "Cry of the People" from *The Giving Earth: A John G. Neihardt Reader* (pp. 17-18), edited and with an introduction by Hilda Neihardt Petri. Copyright © 1991 by the University of Nebraska Press. Used by permission.

JOHN UPDIKE: Interview with National Book Foundation regarding "The Writing Life." Used by permission.